FUTURE U.S. CITIZENS

with Active Book

Sarah Lynn
Federico Salas-Isnardi
Gemma Santos

PEARSON
Longman

Future U.S. Citizens with Active Book

Pearson Education, 10 Bank Street, White Plains, NY 10606

Staff credits: The people who made up the *Future U.S. Citizens with Active Book* team, representing editorial, production, design, manufacturing, and multimedia, are Maretta Callahan, Elizabeth Carlson, Aerin Csigay, Dave Dickey, Christine Edmonds, Nancy Flaggman, Irene Frankel, Shelley Gazes, and Pamela Kohn.

Text composition and design: Word and Image Design Studio, Inc.
Text font: Minion Pro
Cover design: Elizabeth Carlson
Cover photos: Shutterstock.com

Photo credits: Border flag: Shutterstock.com. Page 2 (top) Museum of the City of New York/Corbis, (middle) Shutterstock.com, (bottom) Shutterstock.com; p. 5 (left) The Library of Congress, (right) The Library of Congress; p. 11 Shutterstock.com; p. 13 (left) Shutterstock.com, (right) The Library of Congress; p. 15 The Library of Congress; p. 17 Shutterstock.com; p. 19 (all) Shutterstock.com; p. 21 (left) Shutterstock.com, (right) The Library of Congress; p. 25 The Library of Congress; p. 27 (top) The Library of Congress, (bottom) The Library of Congress; p. 31 (left) The Library of Congress, (right) Shutterstock.com; p. 33 Corbis; p. 35 (top) The Library of Congress, (bottom) Corbis; p. 37 (top) The Library of Congress, (bottom) Shutterstock.com; p. 39 (all) The Library of Congress; p. 41 (left) The Library of Congress, (right) The Library of Congress; p. 45 Isabel Ellsen/Corbis; p. 47 (left) The Library of Congress, (right) Shutterstock.com; p. 49 (left) The Library of Congress, (right) The Library of Congress; p. 53 (left) iStockphoto.com, (right) Jim West/Alamy; p. 55 Shutterstock.com; p. 57 The Library of Congress; p. 59 (top left) Shutterstock.com, (bottom left) Bob Daemmrich/PhotoEdit, Inc., (right) Shutterstock.com; p. 61 Fotolia.com; p. 63 (1) Shutterstock.com, (2) iStockphoto.com, (3) Shutterstock.com; p. 67 (top left) Shutterstock.com, (top right) Rod Lamkey Jr/epa/Corbis, (bottom) AP Images/Pablo Martinez Monsivais; p. 71 (top left) Mark Wilson/Pool/epa/Corbis, (bottom left) Michael Reynolds/epa/Corbis, (right) Dong-Min Jang/Pool/epa/Corbis; p. 73 Chuck Kennedy/Pool/Corbis; p. 75 Allison Shelley/epa/Corbis; p. 77 (left) Juanjo Martin/Pool/epa/Corbis, (right) Digital Press/Newcom; p. 81 Chuck Kennedy/White House/Handout/CNP/Corbis; p. 83 Shutterstock.com; p. 85 (top) Ron Sachs/CNP/Sygma/Corbis, (bottom) The Library of Congress; p. 87 Rainer Jensen/dpa/Corbis; p. 89 (top) The Library of Congress, (bottom) The Library of Congress; p. 91 Shutterstock.com; p. 93 The Library of Congress; p. 95 (top left) Charles O'Rear/Corbis, (top right) Greg Balfour Evans/Alamy, (bottom left) Shutterstock.com, (bottom right) Lawrence Jackson/White House/Handout/The White House/Corbis; p. 97 (top left) Shutterstock.com, (bottom left) Corbis, (right) Ned Frisk Photography/Corbis; p. 99 (top left) Shutterstock.com, (top right) Shutterstock.com, (bottom left) iStockphoto.com, (bottom right) iStockphoto.com; p. 101 (all) Shutterstock.com; p. 103 JPB-1/Alamy; p. 105 (all) Shutterstock.com; p. 107 (left) iStockphoto.com, (top right) Dreamstime.com, (bottom right) iStockphoto.com; p. 109 (top) The Library of Congress, (bottom) SCPhotos/Alamy; p. 111 (left) Frances Roberts/Alamy, (top right) Ralf-Finn Hestoft/Corbis, (bottom right) Shutterstock.com; p. 113 Fotolia.com; p. 117 (left) Shutterstock.com, (right) Shutterstock.com; p. 119 Shutterstock.com; p. 121 (top) The Library of Congress, (bottom) Shutterstock.com; p. 123 (top left) Dennis MacDonald/Alamy, (bottom left) dbimages/Alamy, (right) Shutterstock.com; p. 125 (left) Shutterstock.com, (right) Shutterstock.com; p. 127 (1) Shutterstock.com, (2) Visions of America, LLC/Alamy, (3) Shutterstock.com; p. 129 (left) Corbis Super RF/Alamy, (right) Larry Downing/Reuters/Corbis; p. 177 (top) Shutterstock.com, (middle) Shutterstock.com, (bottom) Shutterstock.com.

Illustration credits: All maps (except page 190) by Mapping Specialists, Limited; diagram on p. 159 by Laurie Conley.

Text credit: The N-400 form that appears on pages 180–189 can be found at www.uscis.gov

Library of Congress Cataloging-in Publication Data

Lynn, Sarah.
  Future U.S. citizens, with Activebook DVD-ROM / Sarah Lynn, Federico Salas-Isnardi, Gemma Santos.
     p. cm.
  Includes bibliographical references.
  ISBN-10: 0-13-138166-0
  ISBN-13: 978-0-13-138166-7
 1. Citizenship—United States—Examinations—Study guides. 2. Citizenship—United States—Examinations, questions, etc. I. Salas-Isnardi, Federico. II. Santos, Gemma, 1960- III. Title.
  JK1758.L96 2011
  323.6076--dc22

                                                                      2010036454

PEARSON LONGMAN ON THE **WEB**

Pearsonlongman.com offers online resources for teachers. Access our Companion Websites, our online catalog, and our local offices around the world.

Visit us at **pearsonlongman.com**.

ISBN 10: 0-13-138166-0
ISBN 13: 978-0-13-138166-7

Printed in the United States of America
1 2 3 4 5 6 7 8 9 10—V064—15 14 13 12 11

CONTENTS

AUTHORS

Sarah Lynn has over 20 years of experience teaching ESL to adults in the United States and overseas. She is an adult ESL teacher trainer and consultant, providing training in such areas as teaching reading, managing the multi-level classroom, and fostering learner independence through goal setting and persistence strategies. She is an author of *Future: English for Results* and has collaborated on numerous other ESL and literacy publications. Sarah manages a blog for teachers at teachertwoteacher.com. Sarah holds a Master's in TESOL from Teachers College, Columbia University.

Federico Salas-Isnardi is an Adult Literacy Specialist for the Texas Center for the Advancement of Literacy and Learning at Texas A&M University. He is also an ESL author, diversity trainer, and adult education leadership consultant. Federico has 22 years of experience as an ESL and GED instructor, professional development specialist, and program administrator at the local and state levels. He holds a Masters degree in applied linguistics from the University of Houston and is pursuing a PhD in adult education at Texas A&M University. Federico became a naturalized U.S. citizen in 1990.

Gemma Santos is an Educational Specialist with Miami-Dade County Public Schools. She has been an instructor in adult education for over 20 years and has collaborated on numerous ESL and citizenship publications. She is a member of the National Social Studies Council and is also currently serving as parliamentarian for Teachers of English for Speakers of Other Languages International (TESOL). Gemma holds a B.A. and M.S. from the University of Miami and a J.D. from Florida State University Law School. She is pursuing a doctoral degree in education at Nova Southeastern University. Gemma became a naturalized U.S. citizen in 1979.

ACKNOWLEDGMENTS

Eleni Adamis Mundelein High School Adult Education Department, Mundelein, IL

Ricardo Aguilar Van Nuys Education Career Center, Woodland, CA

Ana Almklov Socorro Independent School District Community Education, El Paso, Texas

Harriet Bigelow Mundelein Adult Education Program, Grayslake, Illinois

Maria Garcia-Nunez Armwood High School, Tampa, FL

Kristen Gasimov Hogar Immigrant Services, Falls Church, VA

Lucy Nava East Side Adult Education Program / Overfelt Adult Center, San Jose, CA

Yvonne Porras Ysleta Community Learning Center, El Paso, TX

Julie Wakefield Garden Grove Unified School District, Garden Grove, CA

Welcome to *Future U.S. Citizens*

Future U.S. Citizens is a comprehensive test-prep program for adult English learners at high beginning/low intermediate levels who plan to take the naturalization test to become U.S. citizens. *Future U.S. Citizens* contains an Active Book (DVD-ROM) in the back that is a digital version of the entire book. The Active Book also contains resources and interactive practice activities for your students to use on their own.

For a Flash®tour of the *Future U.S. Citizens* Active Book, go to http://futureenglishforresults.com.

For general English skills development, we suggest *Future: English for Results* Level 2 (high beginner) or Level 3 (low intermediate) as perfect partners. To learn more about the *Future: English for Results* suite of products, go to http://futureenglishforresults.com.

About the Naturalization Test

The naturalization test is conducted during an applicant's Eligibility Interview. The test has two parts: a Civics test and an English test.

During the Civics test, the USCIS officer asks ten questions about U.S. history, government and law, U.S. geography, symbols, and holidays. To pass, an applicant must answer six questions correctly. During the English test, applicants must demonstrate the ability to speak, read, and write in English. The speaking test begins in the waiting room when the officer greets the applicant and lasts throughout the interview. For the reading test, the applicant must read a sentence aloud. For the writing test, the applicant must write a dictated sentence. For more information about these tests, see pages 2, 131, and 173.

The scoring guide used by the USCIS can be found on their website, uscis.gov, and as a PDF document in the *Future U.S. Citizens* Active Book Extra Resources.

About the *Future U.S. Citizens* Student Book

Future U.S. Citizens is divided into three parts: Part I Civics Test Prep, Part II Speaking Test Prep, and Part III Reading and Writing Test Prep.

Civics Test Prep

The 32 lessons of this part of the book include the 100 questions and answers students must learn for the Civics test, grouped thematically. Each lesson:
- presents and practices key vocabulary and civics concepts.
- provides reading articles that contain the answers to the civics questions focused on in each lesson.
- directs students to the corresponding reading and writing practice for the lesson.
- provides "Civics in Action" discussion questions to help students internalize the concepts and principles of democracy in the United States.
- connects to interactive practice activities: e-flashcards, record-and-compare exercises, and writing dictation exercises.

Speaking Test Prep

The 20 lessons of this part of the book are video-based, incorporating excerpts from three mock eligibility interviews to illustrate grammar, body language, and speaking strategies. Units 3 and 4 also include explicit pronunciation instruction and practice. All lessons conclude with role play activities to help students build confidence for their own interviews. To maximize the benefit of the role plays, we suggest you ask students to bring a copy of their completed N-400 to class. If they feel uncomfortable sharing their personal information, provide them with a blank copy of the N-400 and ask them to fill it out with made-up information.

Reading and Writing Test Prep

This part of the book provides 64 reading examples and 64 writing examples that correlate with the Civics content and mirror the sentences that applicants will be asked to read and write during their English test.

Lesson planning

Each Civics lesson plus the associated reading and writing practice will take approximately an hour of class time. Each Speaking lesson will take about an hour of class time. We recommend that you include Civics and Speaking lessons in each class; for example, you may want to do two Civics lessons and a Speaking lesson in one three-hour class. We also recommend that you do the lessons for each part in the order they appear.

About the *Future U.S. Citizens* Active Book

The Active Book is a digital version of the entire student book. The Active Book also features:
- Model video interviews
- Interactive practice activities
- Extra resources
- MP3 audio files

Using the Active Book for teaching your class

We encourage you to use the Active Book features of *Future U.S. Citizens* as you teach your class. You will need a computer, external speakers, and an LCD projector with a screen or whiteboard. When you play the Active Book, the pages of the book will be projected onto your screen or whiteboard.

Click directly on ◀)) to play the correct audio track. Click directly on ▮◀ to play the correct video segment. For additional information about the features of the Active Book, go to the "About the Active Book" link from the Active Book Contents screen.

Audio files

We encourage you to use the audio program in class to provide students with exposure to different voices. The entire audio program can be found in the MP3 files in the Active Book. To use the MP3 files in class, you can play them on a computer or you can download the files onto an MP3 player. You will need external speakers if you are using a computer or MP3 player in class.

Using the videos

Three model video interviews in the Active Book illustrate the grammar, vocabulary, and speaking strategies presented and practiced in the Speaking units. You can project the videos directly from the Active Book with an LCD projector. Video scripts are available from the Extra Resources tab on the Active Book. You may want to print out copies of these scripts or have students print them out. Students can refer to them during the Speaking lessons if they need extra support.

Having students use the Active Book outside of class

Three types of interactive practice activities and the mock video interviews provide students with extra practice for all aspects of the naturalization test: the 100 Civics questions, the speaking test, the reading test, and the writing test. Students can do the interactive practice activities in a computer lab, at home, or wherever they have access to a computer. Go to page xix to read more about the interactive practice activities.

Getting the Most From *Future U.S. Citizens*

To help your students get the most from the *Future U.S. Citizens* program:
- Look at the teaching notes on pages ix-xvi, which provide helpful teaching tips for each type of lesson in this book.
- Present the information in *To the Student* on pages xvii and xviii to the class during the first week.
- Review the information for each test prep section on pages 2, 131, and 173 with the class to help familiarize students with the different parts of the tests.
- Show the class the N-400 form and glossary, map of North America, and 100 Civics questions and answers in the back of the student book.
- Point out to students that there are answer keys in the back of the book for the Civics and Speaking sections. The answer key for the Writing section is on pages 178–179.
- Demonstrate how to use the Active Book in class or in the computer lab. Make sure students know how to access all of the interactive practice activities and the model video interviews.
- Also show students the Extra Resources: N-400 form, Video Scripts, USCIS Reading Vocabulary, USCIS Writing Vocabulary, and USCIS Scoring Guidelines.

For answers to all your questions about how to teach with *Future U.S. Citizens*, ask our expert, Sarah Lynn. E-mail Sarah at asksarahlynn@pearson.com

Sarah Lynn teaching at Westchester Community College, New York

In addition, *Symbols of America*, a free set of interactive whiteboard lessons and activities about America's historic national icons, can be found on http://www.pearsoned.com/press/2010/09/07/symbols-of-america-featured-in-free-whiteboard-interactive-lessons-for-elementary-social-studies-classrooms.htm

Part I: Civics Test Prep

The first page of each Civics lesson includes a subset of questions from the 100 Civics questions and a schema-building exercise to provide a framework for the lesson topic. Research shows that when students evaluate their knowledge of a new content area and identify what they need to learn, their comprehension and retention of the new information is greater.

Have students listen to the questions. Play the audio again, pausing after each question. Have students write answers. Then ask the class to share their answers.

Have students write a check (✓) next to the questions and answers they did not know. Tell students that they will read an article that will help them learn more about the questions and answers in this lesson.

On the Active Book screen you will see ▣. Click on the icon to go to the answers.

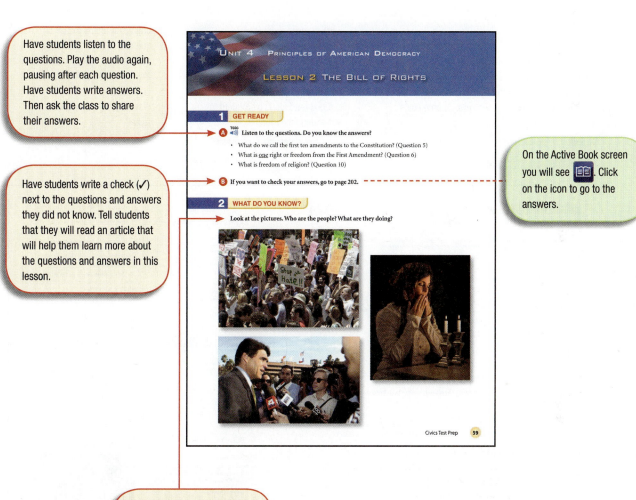

Ask students to say what they see in the pictures. Write the words and phrases on the board. Then have students work in pairs to do the exercise. Go over the answers with the class.

The second page of each Civics lesson includes vocabulary exercises that pre-teach words and concepts before students read the article on the third page. A key word exercise presents important people, places, documents, and events of American history. The article contains the answers to the Civics questions on the first page of the lesson. It frames the information students need to know in an engaging and meaningful way to help them better remember what they learn.

Have students work individually to do the exercise. Encourage them to use context to guess the meaning of the words. Have students work in pairs to compare answers. Then go over the answers with the class.

Play the audio and have students read along silently. Research shows that students can improve their reading fluency by listening to a text read aloud by a fluent and experienced reader.

Engage students by asking questions about the culture note, for example, *Did you know this? Does this information connect to your daily life? What else do you know about this topic?*

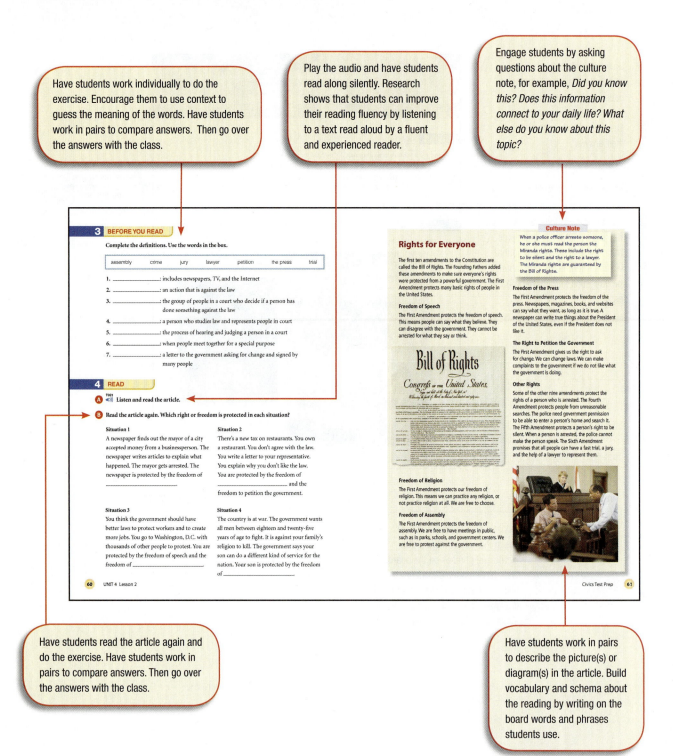

Have students read the article again and do the exercise. Have students work in pairs to compare answers. Then go over the answers with the class.

Have students work in pairs to describe the picture(s) or diagram(s) in the article. Build vocabulary and schema about the reading by writing on the board words and phrases students use.

The last page of each Civics lesson includes a reading comprehension exercise about the article and then a class activity that connects U.S. government and civics to students' everyday lives. Students can prepare for the English test by reading and writing sentences about the lesson topic and doing interactive practice activities on the Active Book.

Have students read the questions first. Then have them re-read the article and do the comprehension exercise. Ask students to work in pairs and compare answers. Then go over the exercise with the class.

---

5 CHECK YOUR UNDERSTANDING

Read the article. Write *T* for True or *F* for False. Then correct the false sentences.

_____ 1. The twenty-seven amendments of the Constitution are the Bill of Rights.

_____ 2. The First Amendment protects freedom of speech, religion, assembly, press, and the right to petition the government.

_____ 3. Freedom of religion means a person can follow any religion or no religion at all.

_____ 4. Freedom of speech means a person can say his or her ideas out loud but not write them.

_____ 5. Freedom of assembly means people can have parties in their homes.

_____ 6. The freedom to petition the government means people can try to change the laws when they don't like them.

_____ 7. Freedom of the press means newspapers and magazines can print false information.

_____ 8. When someone is arrested, the Bill of Rights takes away a person's rights.

6 READ AND WRITE

A READ. Go to page 174. Read sentences 29–30 aloud and check your pronunciation.

B WRITE. Go to page 176. Listen and write sentences 29–30.

7 CIVICS IN ACTION

DISCUSS. What is protected in the Bill of Rights? How can these protections affect your daily life?

Connect to Your Active Book

Use e-flashcards to prepare for the civics test.
Do the record-and-compare exercises to prepare for the reading test.
Do the writing dictation exercises to prepare for the writing test.

Can you...answer the questions on page 59 about the Bill of Rights? ☐

62   UNIT 4 Lesson 2

Have students work in pairs and take turns reading the sentences aloud. Then play the recording and have the class repeat. Help students with pronunciation difficulties.

Play the recording or read aloud from the Writing Answer Key on pages 178 and 179. Have students write the sentences.

Have students discuss the lesson content and connect it to the world they live in. Help students as needed with grammar or vocabulary so they can focus on expressing their ideas.

On the Active Book screen you will see 📖. Click on the icon to go to the Reading and Writing sentences.

On the Active Book screen you will see 📖. Click on the icon to go to the interactive practice activities for the lesson.

Ask the Civics questions on the first page of the lesson. You can also play the audio. Have students write the answers. Then have them go to pages 202–206 to check their answers. Go over the answers with the class. The process of answering and confirming helps students to remember and to reconstruct the information they learned.

Part II: Speaking Test Prep

The Speaking lessons include audio and video segments of mock interviews with three applicants: Maria Rivas, Weimin Gao, and Ekaterina Andropova. Unit 1 reviews grammar students will need for the Civics and English tests. Video segments of the interviews provide models of the grammar points.

On the Active Book screen click on 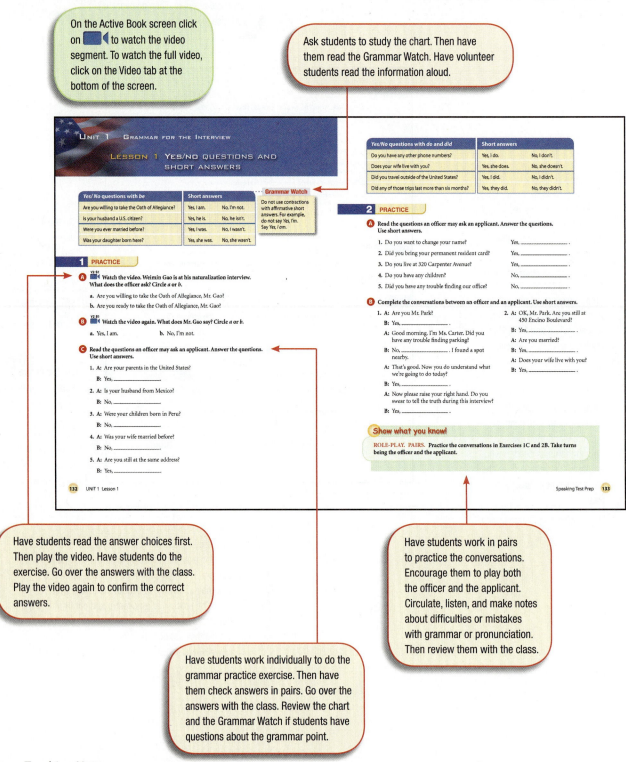 to watch the video segment. To watch the full video, click on the Video tab at the bottom of the screen.

Ask students to study the chart. Then have them read the Grammar Watch. Have volunteer students read the information aloud.

Have students read the answer choices first. Then play the video. Have students do the exercise. Go over the answers with the class. Play the video again to confirm the correct answers.

Have students work in pairs to practice the conversations. Encourage them to play both the officer and the applicant. Circulate, listen, and make notes about difficulties or mistakes with grammar or pronunciation. Then review them with the class.

Have students work individually to do the grammar practice exercise. Then have them check answers in pairs. Go over the answers with the class. Review the chart and the Grammar Watch if students have questions about the grammar point.

Unit 2 focuses on following directions and body language. Video segments of applicant Ekaterina Andropova show what kind of experience students may have at the beginning of the naturalization interview.

Have students read the information silently as you read aloud. Have students read the information silently again and underline any information they didn't know. Call on students to share what they underlined.

Have students predict what they will hear or see in the video. Then play the video and have students check their predictions.

Each lesson in Unit 2 includes an interview strategy. Have students read the strategy and underline any information that is new to them. Then discuss the concepts and any cultural issues with the class.

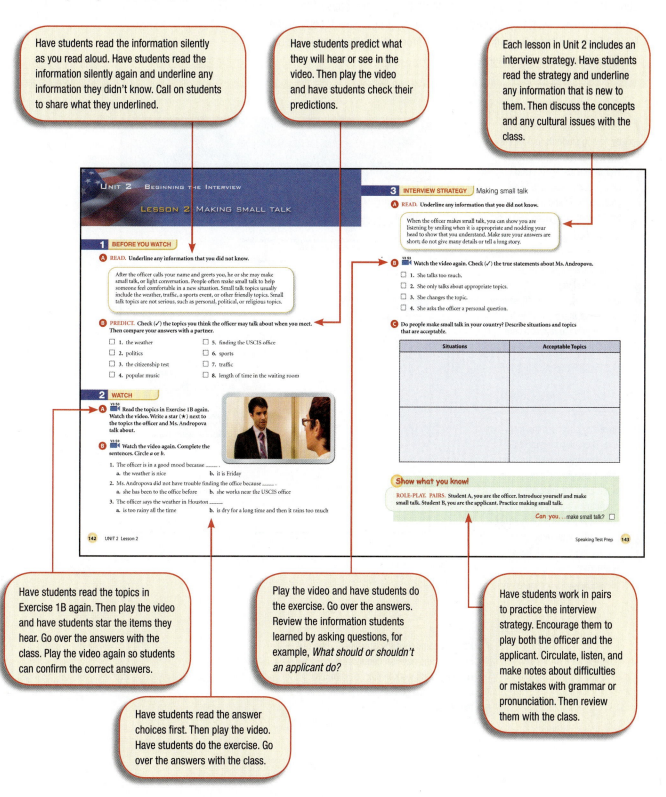

UNIT 2   BEGINNING THE INTERVIEW

LESSON 2   MAKING SMALL TALK

1   BEFORE YOU WATCH

Ⓐ READ. Underline any information that you did not know.

After the officer calls your name and greets you, he or she may make small talk, or light conversation. People often make small talk to help someone feel comfortable in a new situation. Small talk topics usually include the weather, traffic, a sports event, or other friendly topics. Small talk topics are not serious, such as personal, political, or religious topics.

Ⓑ PREDICT. Check (✓) the topics you think the officer may talk about when you meet. Then compare your answers with a partner.

☐ 1. the weather   ☐ 5. finding the USCIS office
☐ 2. politics   ☐ 6. sports
☐ 3. the citizenship test   ☐ 7. traffic
☐ 4. popular music   ☐ 8. length of time in the waiting room

2   WATCH

Ⓐ V3 S3 Read the topics in Exercise 1B again. Watch the video. Write a star (★) next to the topics the officer and Ms. Andropova talk about.

Ⓑ V3 S3 Watch the video again. Complete the sentences. Circle *a* or *b*.

1. The officer is in a good mood because _____ .
   a. the weather is nice   b. it is Friday
2. Ms. Andropova did not have trouble finding the office because _____ .
   a. she has been to the office before   b. she works near the USCIS office
3. The officer says the weather in Houston _____
   a. is too rainy all the time   b. is dry for a long time and then it rains too much

142   UNIT 2 Lesson 2

3   INTERVIEW STRATEGY Making small talk

Ⓐ READ. Underline any information that you did not know.

When the officer makes small talk, you can show you are listening by smiling when it is appropriate and nodding your head to show that you understand. Make sure your answers are short; do not give many details or tell a long story.

Ⓑ V3 S3 Watch the video again. Check (✓) the true statements about Ms. Andropova.

☐ 1. She talks too much.
☐ 2. She only talks about appropriate topics.
☐ 3. She changes the topic.
☐ 4. She asks the officer a personal question.

Ⓒ Do people make small talk in your country? Describe situations and topics that are acceptable.

Situations	Acceptable Topics

Show what you know!

ROLE-PLAY. PAIRS. Student A, you are the officer. Introduce yourself and make small talk. Student B, you are the applicant. Practice making small talk.

Can you...make small talk? ☐

Speaking Test Prep   143

Have students read the topics in Exercise 1B again. Then play the video and have students star the items they hear. Go over the answers with the class. Play the video again so students can confirm the correct answers.

Play the video and have students do the exercise. Go over the answers. Review the information students learned by asking questions, for example, *What should or shouldn't an applicant do?*

Have students work in pairs to practice the interview strategy. Encourage them to play both the officer and the applicant. Circulate, listen, and make notes about difficulties or mistakes with grammar or pronunciation. Then review them with the class.

Have students read the answer choices first. Then play the video. Have students do the exercise. Go over the answers with the class.

Units 3 and 4 focus on speaking strategies and pronunciation. Unit 3 provides practice with the type of questions and information the USCIS officer will ask about in Parts 1–9 on the N-400 form. Unit 4 covers information and questions about Parts 10–14 on the form. Ask students to bring in a copy of their N-400 form. If students want to protect their privacy, print out a blank copy of the N-400 form and have them fill in made-up information. The form is included in the Extra Resources of the Active Book.

Set the context for the lesson by having students look at the appropriate part of the N-400. Words that are specialized or low frequency have been glossed. Have students look at the Glossary on pages 180-189.

Have students work in pairs or small groups to brainstorm questions the USCIS officer may ask about this part of the N-400 form. Circulate to make sure students are on task.

Have students read the question first. Then play the video. Go over the answer with the class. Note: Video scripts are available in the Extra Resources file on the Active Book. Provide copies or have students print them out so they may refer to the scripts as they watch the video segments.

Have students read the questions. Then play the video and have students do the exercise. Have students work in pairs to compare answers. Then go over the answers with the class.

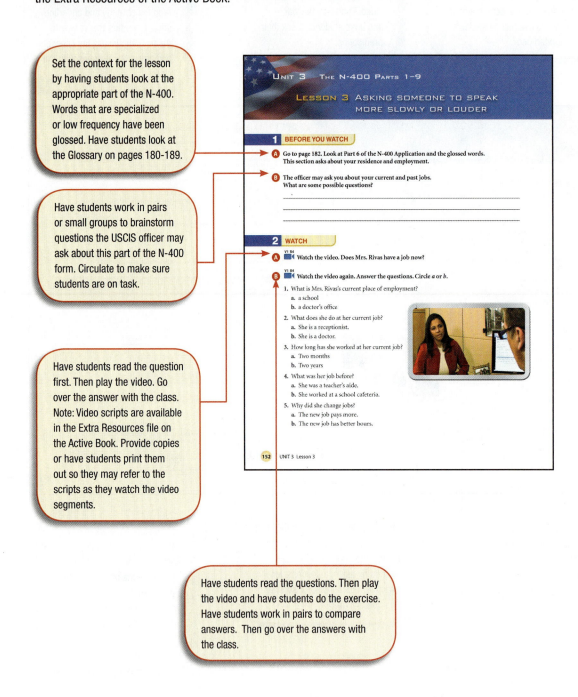

UNIT 3   THE N-400 PARTS 1–9

LESSON 3   ASKING SOMEONE TO SPEAK
MORE SLOWLY OR LOUDER

1   BEFORE YOU WATCH

A   Go to page 182. Look at Part 6 of the N-400 Application and the glossed words. This section asks about your residence and employment.

B   The officer may ask you about your current and past jobs. What are some possible questions?

_____
_____
_____

2   WATCH

A   Watch the video. Does Mrs. Rivas have a job now?

B   Watch the video again. Answer the questions. Circle *a* or *b*.

1. What is Mrs. Rivas's current place of employment?
   a. a school
   b. a doctor's office

2. What does she do at her current job?
   a. She is a receptionist.
   b. She is a doctor.

3. How long has she worked at her current job?
   a. Two months
   b. Two years

4. What was her job before?
   a. She was a teacher's aide.
   b. She worked at a school cafeteria.

5. Why did she change jobs?
   a. The new job pays more.
   b. The new job has better hours.

152   UNIT 3 Lesson 3

Introduce the speaking strategy. Then have students read the information silently. Ask questions to check that students understand the information.

Play the audio. This audio is an excerpt of the video segment students have just watched. Have students answer the question. Then go over the answer with the class.

Say the examples of the speaking strategy aloud to provide a model for correct pronunciation and intonation. Then say the examples again and have students repeat.

Have students read the Pronunciation Watch silently. Then read the Pronunciation Watch aloud while students read along. Ask students to look at the pronunciation examples. If necessary, provide more examples to help students understand.

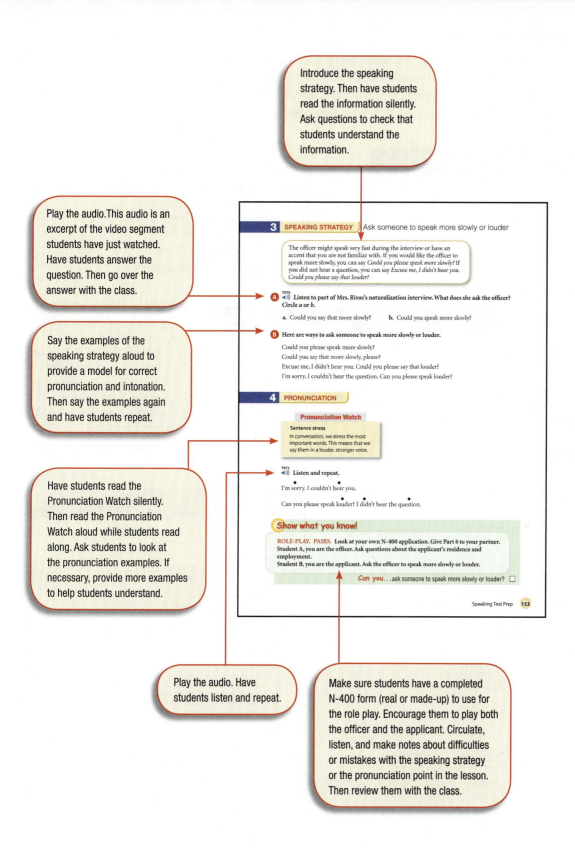

3 SPEAKING STRATEGY | Ask someone to speak more slowly or louder

The officer might speak very fast during the interview or have an accent that you are not familiar with. If you would like the officer to speak more slowly, you can say *Could you please speak more slowly?* If you did not hear a question, you can say *Excuse me, I didn't hear you. Could you please say that louder?*

A T070 Listen to part of Mrs. Rivas's naturalization interview. What does she ask the officer? Circle *a* or *b*.

a. Could you say that more slowly?   b. Could you speak more slowly?

B Here are ways to ask someone to speak more slowly or louder.

Could you please speak more slowly?
Could you say that more slowly, please?
Excuse me, I didn't hear you. Could you please say that louder?
I'm sorry, I couldn't hear the question. Can you please speak louder?

4 PRONUNCIATION

Pronunciation Watch

Sentence stress
In conversation, we stress the most important words. This means that we say them in a louder, stronger voice.

T071 Listen and repeat.

I'm sorry. I couldn't hear you.

Can you please speak louder? I didn't hear the question.

Show what you know!

ROLE-PLAY. PAIRS. Look at your own N-400 application. Give Part 6 to your partner.
Student A, you are the officer. Ask questions about the applicant's residence and employment.
Student B, you are the applicant. Ask the officer to speak more slowly or louder.

Can you... ...ask someone to speak more slowly or louder? ☐

Speaking Test Prep **153**

Play the audio. Have students listen and repeat.

Make sure students have a completed N-400 form (real or made-up) to use for the role play. Encourage them to play both the officer and the applicant. Circulate, listen, and make notes about difficulties or mistakes with the speaking strategy or the pronunciation point in the lesson. Then review them with the class.

Part III: Reading and Writing Test Prep

To prepare for reading during the English test, have students practice by reading sentences aloud and checking their pronunciation. To prepare for writing during the English test, have students practice by listening to dictated sentences, writing them, and then checking their answers. The sentences in both sections are about U.S. history and government.

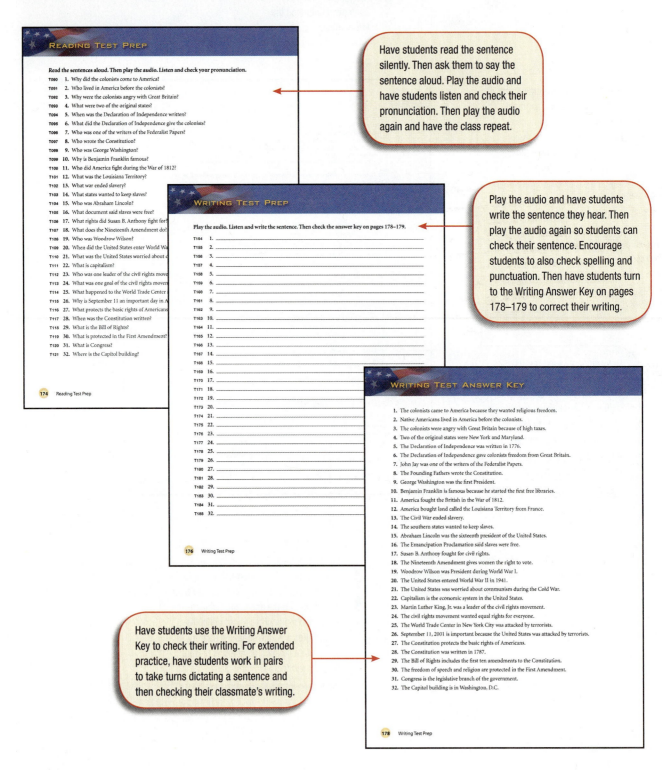

Have students read the sentence silently. Then ask them to say the sentence aloud. Play the audio and have students listen and check their pronunciation. Then play the audio again and have the class repeat.

Play the audio and have students write the sentence they hear. Then play the audio again so students can check their sentence. Encourage students to also check spelling and punctuation. Then have students turn to the Writing Answer Key on pages 178–179 to correct their writing.

Have students use the Writing Answer Key to check their writing. For extended practice, have students work in pairs to take turns dictating a sentence and then checking their classmate's writing.

READING TEST PREP

Read the sentences aloud. Then play the audio. Listen and check your pronunciation.

T090   1. Why did the colonists come to America?
T091   2. Who lived in America before the colonists?
T092   3. Why were the colonists angry with Great Britain?
T093   4. What were two of the original states?
T094   5. When was the Declaration of Independence written?
T095   6. What did the Declaration of Independence give the colonists?
T096   7. Who was one of the writers of the Federalist Papers?
T097   8. Who wrote the Constitution?
T098   9. Who was George Washington?
T099   10. Why is Benjamin Franklin famous?
T100   11. Who did America fight during the War of 1812?
T101   12. What was the Louisiana Territory?
T102   13. What war ended slavery?
T103   14. What states wanted to keep slaves?
T104   15. Who was Abraham Lincoln?
T105   16. What document said slaves were free?
T106   17. What rights did Susan B. Anthony fight for?
T107   18. What does the Nineteenth Amendment do?
T108   19. Who was Woodrow Wilson?
T109   20. When did the United States enter World War
T110   21. What was the United States worried about
T111   22. What is capitalism?
T112   23. Who was one leader of the civil rights move
T113   24. What was one goal of the civil rights movem
T114   25. What happened to the World Trade Center
T115   26. Why is September 11 an important day in A
T116   27. What protects the basic rights of Americans
T117   28. When was the Constitution written?
T118   29. What is the Bill of Rights?
T119   30. What is protected in the First Amendment?
T120   31. What is Congress?
T121   32. Where is the Capitol building?

174   Reading Test Prep

WRITING TEST PREP

Play the audio. Listen and write the sentence. Then check the answer key on pages 178–179.

T154   1. _____
T155   2. _____
T156   3. _____
T157   4. _____
T158   5. _____
T159   6. _____
T160   7. _____
T161   8. _____
T162   9. _____
T163   10. _____
T164   11. _____
T165   12. _____
T166   13. _____
T167   14. _____
T168   15. _____
T169   16. _____
T170   17. _____
T171   18. _____
T172   19. _____
T173   20. _____
T174   21. _____
T175   22. _____
T176   23. _____
T177   24. _____
T178   25. _____
T179   26. _____
T180   27. _____
T181   28. _____
T182   29. _____
T183   30. _____
T184   31. _____
T185   32. _____

176   Writing Test Prep

WRITING TEST ANSWER KEY

1. The colonists came to America because they wanted religious freedom.
2. Native Americans lived in America before the colonists.
3. The colonists were angry with Great Britain because of high taxes.
4. Two of the original states were New York and Maryland.
5. The Declaration of Independence was written in 1776.
6. The Declaration of Independence gave colonists freedom from Great Britain.
7. John Jay was one of the writers of the Federalist Papers.
8. The Founding Fathers wrote the Constitution.
9. George Washington was the first President.
10. Benjamin Franklin is famous because he started the first free libraries.
11. America fought the British in the War of 1812.
12. America bought land called the Louisiana Territory from France.
13. The Civil War ended slavery.
14. The southern states wanted to keep slaves.
15. Abraham Lincoln was the sixteenth president of the United States.
16. The Emancipation Proclamation said slaves were free.
17. Susan B. Anthony fought for civil rights.
18. The Nineteenth Amendment gives women the right to vote.
19. Woodrow Wilson was President during World War I.
20. The United States entered World War II in 1941.
21. The United States was worried about communism during the Cold War.
22. Capitalism is the economic system in the United States.
23. Martin Luther King, Jr. was a leader of the civil rights movement.
24. The civil rights movement wanted equal rights for everyone.
25. The World Trade Center in New York City was attacked by terrorists.
26. September 11, 2001 is important because the United States was attacked by terrorists.
27. The Constitution protects the basic rights of Americans.
28. The Constitution was written in 1787.
29. The Bill of Rights includes the first ten amendments to the Constitution.
30. The freedom of speech and religion are protected in the First Amendment.
31. Congress is the legislative branch of the government.
32. The Capitol building is in Washington, D.C.

178   Writing Test Prep

Congratulations on your decision to become a U.S. citizen! The following is a description of the citizenship application process and the naturalization test. To get complete information, please go to the official United States Citizenship and Immigration Services (USCIS) website at http://www.uscis.gov.

The N-400 Application Form

- Make sure to fill out the form completely.
- Determine which documents you need to submit with your application.
- You will need a copy of your Permanent Resident card, both front and back.
- When you are ready to submit your application, check that you have included the required documents, two passport-style color photographs, and the fee.
- The USCIS will notify you to have your fingerprints taken and sent in.
- The USCIS sends your fingerprints to the Federal Bureau of Investigation (FBI), which conducts a background check.

About the Eligibility Interview

- As part of your application process, you will have an eligibility interview. The USCIS will send you the date, time, and location of the interview. It is important that you notify the USCIS immediately if you change your address.
- It is important that you can attend the interview on the date you are assigned. To reschedule and receive a new date can take many months.

Getting Ready for the Eligibility Interview

- Make sure you prepare and collect any official documents you will need *before* your eligibility interview. If you need to request a document from a government office or even from another country, this will take time. All documents must be in English. If necessary, you will need to have a certified English translator prepare any translations.
- You should visit the testing location before the day of your interview appointment so that you will be familiar with the flow of traffic and the parking arrangements.

Tips for a successful interview

- It's natural to be nervous! You will feel more relaxed if you prepare in advance.
- Get a good night's sleep the night before your interview.
- Keep your energy up. Eat something before you leave home.
- Speak as clearly as you can. The officer knows you may not pronounce every word perfectly.
- Don't worry. It's OK to ask the officer to repeat something if you don't understand.

At the Eligibility Interview

- Be sure to arrive at the interview location earlier than your scheduled appointment. You will need time to pass through a security checkpoint and find the correct room. Do not bring any items that might prevent you from successfully passing through a security checkpoint such as a cell phone, electronic items, or sharp objects.
- You will need to sign in and wait for the USCIS officer to call your name. The officer will greet you and take you to an office. You will be asked to raise your right hand and take an oath to tell the truth.
- During the interview, you will be asked about the information on your N-400 form and your willingness to take an Oath of Allegiance to the United States.
- You will take a Civics test and an English test (speaking, reading, and writing tests). Go to pages 2, 131, and 173 to read about each test.
- Go to www.uscis.gov/citizenship to find out more and to learn about exceptions and accommodations for the interview and tests.
- At the end of the interview, the officer will ask you to sign your application indicating that everything you wrote in the application is the truth. You will also need to sign the two photos you brought.

The Decision

- After your interview, you will receive a form that identifies the status of your application.
- *Granted* means it was approved and you will become an American citizen.
- *Continued* means you need to submit more information or you may not have passed the English test or Civics test.
- *Denied* means it has been rejected. If your application has been denied, the USCIS will send you a notice explaining why.

The Oath

- If your application is granted, you will need to attend a formal naturalization ceremony.
- At the ceremony, you will take an Oath of Allegiance to the United States. Note that even if your application has been granted, you will not be an American citizen until you take the Oath of Allegiance.

The bound-in Active Book includes three types of interactive practice activities:

- E-flashcards to help you prepare for the Civics test
- Record-and-compare exercises to help you prepare for the reading test
- Writing dictation exercises to help you prepare for the writing test

You can access lesson-specific activities from the Connect to Your Active Book section of each Civics lesson. You can also access all of the activities from the tabs at the bottom of the screen.

For a Flash®tour of the *Future U.S. Citizens* Active Book go to http://futureenglishforresults.com.

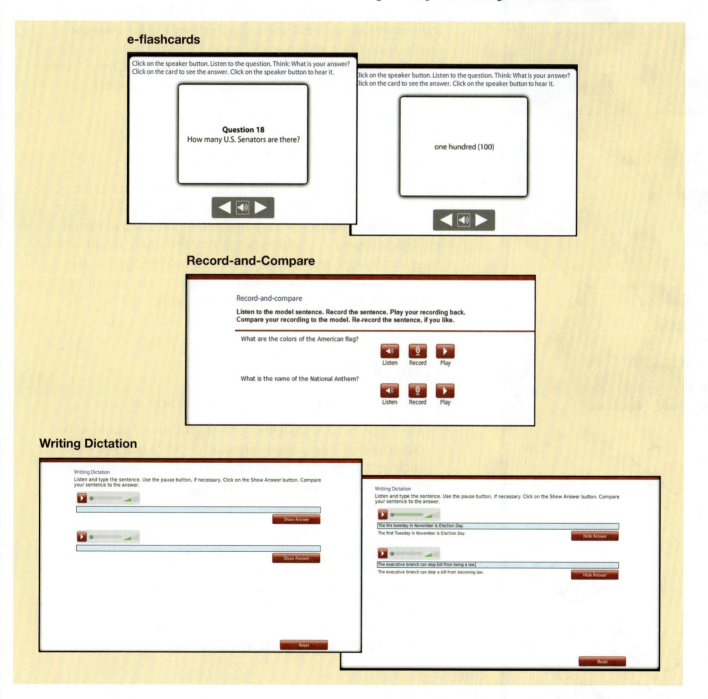

OVERVIEW

During your interview, the officer will ask you 10 civics questions. To pass, you must answer six questions correctly. The officer may not need to ask you all 10 questions!

The 10 questions are taken from the USCIS list of 100 questions and answers about American civics, history, and government. The 100 questions and answers can be found on pages 202-206. Note: If you qualify, you may be eligible to take the Civics Test in your native language with the assistance of an interpreter.

FUTURE U.S. CITIZENS: THE STUDENT BOOK

Part 1 Civics Test Prep contains 32 Civics lessons. The lesson topics cover principles of American democracy, the U.S. system of government, rights and responsibilities, the colonial period and U.S. independence, the expansion of the 1800s, recent American history, important historical information, as well as geography, national symbols, and holidays. All 100 questions and answers are taught in this part of the book.

FUTURE U.S. CITIZENS: THE ACTIVE BOOK

Use the *Future U.S. Citizens* Active Book to help you study.

- The entire book is in digital form on the Active Book, so you can read the Civics lessons on a computer. When you see 🔊, click on it to play the audio files for the Civics questions and the reading articles. When you see 📖, click on it to go to other screens.

- The Active Book contains interactive practice activities. To help you prepare for the Civics test, there are e-flashcards for all of the 100 questions and answers. Use the e-flashcards to help you understand the concepts and remember the questions and answers. You can go to the e-flashcards from the last screen of each Civics lesson. You can also click on the e-flashcards tab at the bottom of each screen.

LESSON 1   EARLY AMERICA

1   GET READY

A 🔊 **T002** **Listen to the questions. Do you know the answers?**

- What is <u>one</u> reason colonists came to America? (Question 58)
- Who lived in America before the Europeans arrived? (Question 59)
- Name <u>one</u> American Indian tribe in the United States. (Question 87)

B **If you want to check your answers, go to pages 204 and 205.**

2   WHAT DO YOU KNOW?

Look at the map. Point to the state where you live now. Name Native American tribe(s) in your state.

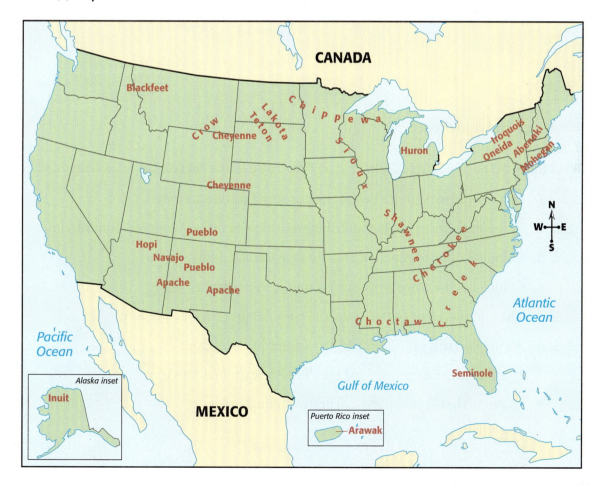

Do you know the words in bold? What do they mean? Circle *a* or *b*.

1. In the United States, people can **practice** any religion.
   a. follow
   b. take

2. Each Native American **tribe** in North America speaks a different language.
   a. group of people
   b. group of businesses

3. All American citizens have the **political liberty** to say what they believe.
   a. political freedom
   b. political party

4. The first **colony** in America was Jamestown, Virginia.
   a. large state in a region
   b. land ruled by another country

5. The first **colonists** in America came from England.
   a. people who live in a colony
   b. people who work on farms

6. Many people come to the United States for a better life. They often come for **economic opportunity** because there are no jobs at home.
   a. the chance to make money
   b. the chance to move

7. In Europe, some people were afraid of **persecution** because they had different beliefs.
   a. being moved
   b. being hurt

8. In the 1600s, life in America was very hard. Only a few people **survived**.
   a. lived
   b. died

4 **READ**

A T003 🔊)) Listen and read the article.

B Read the article again. Write *T* for True or *F* for False. Then correct the false sentences.

_____ 1. People lived in America before the European colonists arrived.

_____ 2. Three large American Indian tribes were the Cherokee, Seminole, and Pilgrims.

_____ 3. Colonists came to America because they wanted political liberty.

_____ 4. Colonists left Europe to escape economic opportunity.

_____ 5. The Pilgrims came to the American colonies for religious freedom.

_____ 6. All the Pilgrims survived their first winter in America.

_____ 7. The Native Americans helped the Pilgrims learn how to survive.

_____ 8. The first Thanksgiving was celebrated in England.

A New Land

Native Americans

Native Americans, or American Indians, lived in North America for thousands of years before the Europeans arrived. Some of the largest tribes, or groups, were the Cherokee, Seminole, and Sioux. Each tribe had its own language and way of life. For Native Americans, land was important. They took care of the land.

Economic Opportunity

In the 1600s and 1700s, Europeans came to America to start a new life. They came for many reasons. Some came for economic opportunity. They came to start businesses in the colonies. Others came to start their own farms. In Europe there was not enough land for all the people, but North America had a lot of land. The new world promised opportunity for people ready to work hard.

Liberty

Many colonists came to the new world because it offered freedom. Some wanted to practice their own religion. Others wanted political liberty to disagree with their government. In their home countries, some were punished for thinking differently or following a different religion. They came to America to escape persecution, to live in peace, and to be free to follow their beliefs.

Colonists and Native Americans

The Pilgrims

One group of English colonists was called the Pilgrims. They came to America to find religious freedom. They did not want to practice the religion of their King and decided to go to America. The Pilgrims came to America in November of 1620. They arrived in a place now called Massachusetts.

The Pilgrims arrived much farther north than they had planned. They were not ready for the hard northern winter and did not know how to survive. Half of their people died during that first winter.

The first Thanksgiving, 1621

Then the Pilgrims made friends with the Native Americans. The Abenaki tribe showed these new colonists how to survive in their new land. In their second November, the Pilgrims invited all of their Native American neighbors to share a meal. They thanked the Native Americans for their help. This was the first Thanksgiving.

Culture Note

Many U.S. state names are Native American words. Oklahoma is a Choctaw Indian word meaning "red people." Kentucky is from an Iroquoian word meaning "land of tomorrow." Ohio is from an Iroquoian word meaning "great river."

5   CHECK YOUR UNDERSTANDING

Read the article. Write the reasons in the correct column.

| economic opportunity | freedom | land | persecution |
| political liberty | political problems | religious freedom | |

People Left Europe to Escape	People Came to America to Have

6   READ AND WRITE

A   READ.   Go to page 174. Read sentences 1–2 aloud and check your pronunciation.

B   WRITE.   Go to page 176. Listen and write sentences 1–2.

7   CIVICS IN ACTION

DISCUSS.   **Many immigrants come to the United States because it offers freedom. Why did you or people you know come?**

Connect to Your Active Book

Use e-flashcards to prepare for the civics test.

Do the record-and-compare exercises to prepare for the reading test.

Do the writing dictation exercises to prepare for the writing test.

Can you...answer the questions on page 3 about early America? ☐

Lesson 2 The American Revolution

1 GET READY

A T004 🔊)) Listen to the questions. Do you know the answers?

- Why did the colonists fight the British? (Question 61)
- There were thirteen original states. Name <u>three</u>. (Question 64)

B If you want to check your answers, go to page 204.

2 WHAT DO YOU KNOW?

Look at the map. What do you notice about the thirteen colonies?

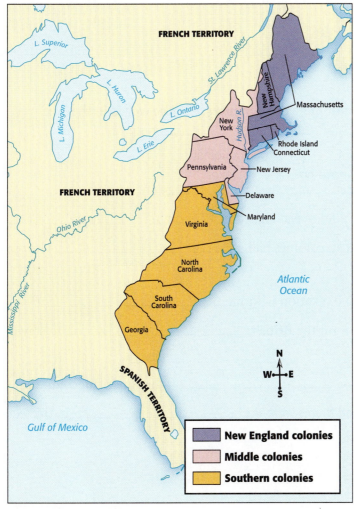

The thirteen original colonies

3 BEFORE YOU READ

A Match the words and the definitions.

_____ 1. army   **a.** a person who speaks for a group of people

_____ 2. soldier   **b.** a voice in an organization or government

_____ 3. representative   **c.** the military on land

_____ 4. representation   **d.** a person who fights in the military

B Complete the definitions. Use the words in the box.

| laws | original | self-government | taxes |

1. _____: when people control their own community or state

2. _____: money collected by the government for different purposes

3. _____: the first of something

4. _____: government rules that everyone follows

4 READ

A T005 🔊 Listen and read the article.

B Read the article again. Then complete the sentences. Use the words in the box.

| army | July 4 | original |
| representation | self-government | taxes |

1. The Declaration of Independence was signed in 1776 on _____.

2. Until the 1760s, the American colonies had _____. They made their own laws.

3. American colonists said, "No taxation without _____."

4. American colonists didn't want the British _____ to stay in their homes.

5. Great Britain put high _____ on the American colonies.

6. The first states in the United States were the _____ thirteen colonies.

The Colonies Grow into a Country

For the first 140 years, the American colonies got along with Great Britain. Great Britain gave the colonies freedom to make many of their own laws and run their own governments. They had self-government. The colonists did not have political representation in the British government, but that was not a problem. Their own colonial governments worked well and they were busy building their new lives in a new world.

High Taxes

In the 1760s, Great Britain decided to take more control over its American colonies. First, Great Britain increased taxes. The high taxes made the colonists angry. They said, "We want representation in the British government. We want to vote on tax laws. No taxation without representation!"

The British Army

Then Great Britain sent more soldiers to the colonies. It told the colonists to give housing and food to the army. The colonists didn't want the British army to stay in their homes. Tensions between British soldiers and American colonists were very high.

The Colonists Fight the British

In the colony of Massachusetts, the colonists organized against the British. They did not buy anything British. They didn't even drink tea because it was British. They attacked businesses that sold anything British. Then they attacked a boat carrying a shipment of British tea.

In 1775, Great Britain shut down the colonial government in Massachusetts. On April 17, 1775, in the small town of Lexington outside of Boston, some colonists and British soldiers started fighting. This was the beginning of the American Revolutionary War.

Three weeks later, in May 1775, representatives from all thirteen colonies met in Philadelphia. They talked about how to fight against the British. They started an army and asked George Washington to be the leader. They were fighting for representation in the British government and self-government.

The Declaration of Independence

After a year of war, the colonies wanted to be an independent country. On July 4, 1776, representatives from all thirteen colonies signed the Declaration of Independence. This day changed the war. Now the colonies were fighting to become the United States of America. Seven years later, in 1783, they finally won the war. Great Britain ended its control of the American colonies. A new country was born.

Battles during the Revolutionary War

5 CHECK YOUR UNDERSTANDING

Read the article. Number the events to put them in time order.

____ **a.** Great Britain closes Massachusetts' self-government.

____ **b.** Great Britain puts high taxes on the colonies.

__1__ **c.** Great Britain gives the American colonies a lot of freedom.

____ **d.** Great Britain sends more soldiers to the American colonies.

____ **e.** The British army and American colonists start fighting.

____ **f.** People in Massachusetts stop buying anything British.

____ **g.** Great Britain says soldiers can live in colonists' homes.

6 READAND WRITE

A READ. Go to page 174. Read sentences 3–4 aloud and check your pronunciation.

B WRITE. Go to page 176. Listen and write sentences 3–4.

7 CIVICS IN ACTION

DISCUSS. **What is the history of your country's independence? Who were some of the people who helped your country win independence?**

Connect to Your Active Book

Use e-flashcards to prepare for the civics test.

Do the record-and-compare exercises to prepare for the reading test.

Do the writing dictation exercises to prepare for the writing test.

Can you...answer the questions on page 7 about the American Revolution? ☐

LESSON 3 THE DECLARATION OF INDEPENDENCE

1   GET READY

A T006 🔊 **Listen to the questions. Do you know the answers?**

- What did the Declaration of Independence do? (Question 8)
- What are <u>two</u> rights in the Declaration of Independence? (Question 9)
- Who wrote the Declaration of Independence? (Question 62)
- When was the Declaration of Independence adopted? (Question 63)

B If you want to check your answers, go to pages 202 and 204.

2   WHAT DO YOU KNOW?

Look at the picture. Who are these men? Why are they important in U.S. history?

Benjamin Franklin, John Adams, and Thomas Jefferson

Do you know the words in bold? What do the sentences mean? Circle *a* or *b*.

1. Citizens have the **right** to vote.
    a. Citizens must vote.
    b. Citizens can vote if they want to.

2. All people are **equal** according to the law.
    a. All people have different rights according to the law.
    b. All people have the same rights according to the law.

3. The law was **adopted** by the people.
    a. The people accepted the law and followed it.
    b. The people said they didn't like the law.

4. Parents **protect** their children from danger.
    a. Parents keep their children safe.
    b. Parents put their children in danger.

5. The colonists **declared independence** from Great Britain.
    a. The colonists said to the world, "We are not a part of Great Britain!"
    b. The colonists said to the world, "We want to stay a part of Great Britain!"

4 READ

A 🔊 **T007 Listen and read the article.**

B Read the article again. Then complete the paragraph. Use the words in the box.

equal	government	independent	liberty	rights

On July 4, 1776, the United States became (**1**)_____ of Great Britain. The
Declaration of Independence said that all people are (**2**)_____ . All people have
the right to life, (**3**) _____ , and the pursuit of happiness. The people can change
their (**4**)_____ if they are not happy with how it is working. A government
cannot take away the basic (**5**)_____ of the people.

The Declaration of Independence

Culture Note

A seamstress named Betsy Ross was asked to make the first American flag. She finished the flag in time for the first reading of the Declaration of Independence on July 4, 1776.

After a year of fighting against Great Britain, the American colonies realized they did not just want representation in the British government. They wanted to have their own government and their own country.

Thomas Jefferson

The thirteen colonies needed to tell Great Britain they wanted independence and why. They asked a lawyer from Virginia, Thomas Jefferson, to help write a declaration. He was a great writer and thinker. On July 4, 1776, representatives from all thirteen colonies adopted the Declaration of Independence. That day they declared their freedom from Great Britain. Today, we still celebrate July 4 as an important American holiday. We call it Independence Day.

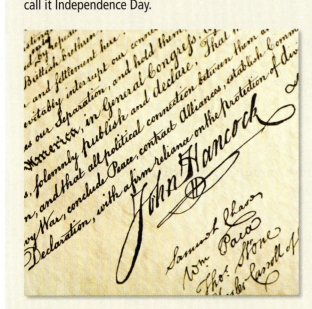

Basic Rights

The Declaration of Independence is important for two reasons. First, it announced our independence from Great Britain. It declared that the United States was free of Great Britain.

Second, it explained the reason the colonies wanted independence. It said that all people are equal, and all people have basic rights. They have the rights to life, liberty, and the pursuit of happiness. No government can take away these rights. When a government does not protect these basic rights, the people can change their government. The colonies started their own government because the British government did not respect the colonists' rights to life, liberty, and the pursuit of happiness.

In the Declaration of Independence, Jefferson wrote about a government that belongs to the people. He said a government's job is to protect people's basic rights. These are the key ideas that formed the United States government.

Culture Note

John Hancock was a representative from Massachusetts. He wrote his name in large letters on the Declaration of Independence. Hancock wanted the king of England to know that he was not afraid. Today if someone asks you to "sign your John Hancock," the person wants you to sign your full name.

5 CHECK YOUR UNDERSTANDING

Read the article. Write *T* for True or *F* for False. Then correct the false sentences.

_____ 1. John Hancock wrote the Declaration of Independence.

_____ 2. The Declaration of Independence was adopted on July 4, 1766.

_____ 3. July 4 is called Declaration Day.

_____ 4. The Declaration of Independence said that the United States is free from Great Britain.

_____ 5. The Declaration of Independence said that all people have the right to life, liberty, and dependence.

_____ 6. The colonists started their own government because the British government did not respect their rights.

_____ 7. Jefferson said the job of the government is to protect people's jobs.

6 READ AND WRITE

A **READ.** Go to page 174. Read sentences 5–6 aloud and check your pronunciation.

B **WRITE.** Go to page 176. Listen and write sentences 5–6.

7 CIVICS IN ACTION

DISCUSS. Are there July 4 celebrations in your community? Describe ways people in the United States celebrate Independence Day.

Connect to Your Active Book

Use e-flashcards to prepare for the civics test.

Do the record-and-compare exercises to prepare for the reading test.

Do the writing dictation exercises to prepare for the writing test.

*Can you...*answer the questions on page 11 about the Declaration of Independence? ☐

1 GET READY

A T008 🔊 **Listen to the questions. Do you know the answers?**

- What happened at the Constitutional Convention? (Question 65)
- When was the Constitution written? (Question 66)
- The Federalist Papers supported the passage of the U.S. Constitution. Name <u>one</u> of the writers. (Question 67)

B **If you want to check your answers, go to page 204.**

2 WHAT DO YOU KNOW?

Look at the picture. Describe this meeting. What do you think is happening?

The Constitutional Convention, 1787

Do you know the words in bold? What do they mean? Circle *a* or *b*.

1. Some colonists didn't want independence from Great Britain. They **supported** the British.

   a. agreed with   **b.** disagreed with

2. In 1783, the United States of America was a new **nation**.

   a. country   **b.** city

3. The **passage** of the Constitution took a year and a half.

   a. voting yes on a law   **b.** voting no on a law

4. In the United States, the central government and the states **share** power. The states can make many of their own laws.

   a. divide   **b.** control

5. The United States has a **federal** government that works together with the states. This government leads the whole nation.

   a. free   **b.** central

4 READ

T009

A 🔊) Listen and read the article.

B Read the article again. Answer the questions. Circle *a*, *b*, or *c*.

1. Where was the Constitutional Convention?
   a. Philadelphia   **b.** Washington, D.C.   **c.** Boston

2. When was the Constitutional Convention?
   a. 1783   **b.** 1787   **c.** 1788

3. When was the passage of the U.S. Constitution?
   a. 1787   **b.** 1788   **c.** 1789

4. Which government did the representatives at the Constitutional Convention think should be the strongest?
   a. state   **b.** federal   **c.** the king

5. What does the Bill of Rights protect?
   a. the people   **b.** the U.S. Constitution   **c.** the representatives

6. Who was one of the Founding Fathers?
   a. Publius   **b.** John Jay   **c.** Great Britain

One Nation—Thirteen States

When the American Revolutionary War ended in 1783, the United States of America was one nation with thirteen independent states. Each state was part of the United States, but had its own government. In 1783, the federal government was very weak. The states didn't want a strong central government at that time. They had just fought a long war with Great Britain to be free of a central power. But as time went by, the state governments realized they needed a stronger federal government.

Constitutional Convention

In 1787, representatives from each state went to Philadelphia, Pennsylvania, for the Constitutional Convention. They worked together for four months to write the Constitution of the United States of America. This Constitution set up the federal government of the United States.

Federalist Papers

Each state had to vote on the passage of the Constitution. Newspapers printed the Constitution for everyone to read. Many people didn't like it. They said, "The federal government is our new king! It takes the power away from the states! We will lose our rights!"

James Madison, John Jay, and Alexander Hamilton were members of the Constitutional Convention. They believed that a strong federal government was the only way for the young nation to survive. They wrote articles in the newspapers to support the passage of the Constitution. Their eighty-five writings are called the Federalist Papers because they supported a strong federal government. All three men signed their writings with the name *Publius* because they wanted to keep their real names a secret. Students of law still study the Federalist Papers today to better understand the U.S. Constitution.

The Bill of Rights

In 1788, enough states voted for the Constitution to make it the law. But many people were still worried the new central government would take away their rights. In 1789, the representatives added the Bill of Rights to the Constitution. It protects people's right to speak out, to practice their religion, to change laws, and to have meetings. It also protects people when they are arrested.

The Founding Fathers

The Declaration of Independence, the Constitution, and the Bill of Rights were written by men we now call the Founding Fathers. These men created the first nation in the world to declare independence from a colonial power. They helped write the U.S. Constitution, which is the oldest constitution in use in the world today.

The Declaration of Independence

Culture Note

Madison, Jay, and Hamilton chose the name *Publius* in honor of an ancient Roman man, who helped his people.

5 CHECK YOUR UNDERSTANDING

Read the article. Number the events to put them in time order.

_____ **a.** At first, the states wanted freedom from a strong government.

__1__ **b.** The United States won the war against Great Britain.

_____ **c.** The newspapers printed the Constitution for people to read.

_____ **d.** Representatives met at the Constitutional Convention to write the Constitution.

_____ **e.** Then some Americans realized they needed a stronger federal government.

_____ **f.** Enough states passed the Constitution. It became the law.

_____ **g.** Publius wrote newspaper articles supporting the Constitution.

_____ **h.** Later, the representatives added the Bill of Rights to the Constitution.

6 READ AND WRITE

A READ. Go to page 174. Read sentences 7–8 aloud and check your pronunciation.

B WRITE. Go to page 176. Listen and write sentences 7–8.

7 CIVICS IN ACTION

DISCUSS. The Bill of Rights is connected to our everyday lives. For example, we can practice the religion we want to. Can you give more examples?

Connect to Your Active Book

Use e-flashcards to prepare for the civics test.

Do the record-and-compare exercises to prepare for the reading test.

Do the writing dictation exercises to prepare for the writing test.

Can you...answer the questions on page 15 about the Constitution? ☐

Lesson 5 George Washington and Benjamin Franklin

1 GET READY

A T010 🔊 Listen to the questions. Do you know the answers?

- What is <u>one</u> thing Benjamin Franklin is famous for? (Question 68)
- Who is the "Father of Our Country"? (Question 69)
- Who was the first president? (Question 70)

B If you want to check your answers, go to pages 204 and 205.

2 WHAT DO YOU KNOW?

A Look at the stamps and bills. Point to George Washington. Point to Benjamin Franklin.

B Why are these men on U.S. stamps and bills?

A Read the sentences. Do you know the words in bold?

1. There are many **battles** in a war.
2. The United States is represented by **diplomats** in many countries.
3. In 2008, America **elected** Barak Obama, the first African American to be president.
4. The president of the United States **leads** the government.
5. There were fifty-five **members** of the Constitutional Convention.
6. The **Postmaster General** makes sure that mail service is good throughout the United States and also to other countries.

B Match the words and the definitions.

_____ 1. battle   **a.** to choose by voting

_____ 2. diplomat   **b.** a short fight between military groups

_____ 3. elect   **c.** the person who manages the U.S. Postal Service

_____ 4. lead   **d.** a person who helps solve problems between countries

_____ 5. member   **e.** to direct a group of people

_____ 6. Postmaster General   **f.** a person in a group

4 READ

A 🔊 **T011** Listen and read the article.

B Read the article again. Then complete the sentences. Use the words in the box.

diplomat	Constitutional Convention	Father of Our Country
Poor Richard's Almanac	Postmaster General	President

1. Both Benjamin Franklin and George Washington were members of the
_____.

2. Benjamin Franklin was a U.S. _____ in England and in France.

3. George Washington was the first _____ of the United States.

4. Benjamin Franklin was the first _____ of the United States.

5. George Washington is called the _____.

6. Benjamin Franklin wrote the magazine called _____.

America's First Leaders

George Washington

Americans call George Washington the Father of Our Country. He was born in Virginia in 1732. As a young man he was a soldier in the French-Indian War, but then he became a farmer. For many years he lived happily on his large farm in Virginia with his wife, Martha. During this time he also served as a representative in Virginia's colonial government.

In 1775, George Washington became the leader of the colonial army in the American Revolutionary War against Great Britain. Washington had to organize and train thousands of farmers and other ordinary men to become soldiers. Washington realized very soon that his group of men could never win in a traditional war against Great Britain. So he planned and fought small surprise battles against the British. In 1783, he surprised the world by winning the war against Great Britain.

After the war, Washington returned to his quiet life on his farm. In 1787, Washington became worried that the thirteen states would turn into thirteen different nations. He knew the young United States of America needed a national constitution, so he left his farm to lead the Constitutional Convention in Philadelphia. For four long months, he worked with the other Founding Fathers to write the Constitution.

The new constitution called for a President. In 1789, George Washington took office as the first President of the United States of America. He is the only President in American history to be elected unanimously. Everyone wanted him to be the president. After completing eight years in office, he returned to his farm. In 1799, he died a farmer and a hero of the nation.

Washington crossing the Delaware River with his army in 1776.

Benjamin Franklin

Another important person who helped write the U.S. Constitution was Benjamin Franklin. At the age of seventy-seven, he was the oldest member at the Constitutional Convention. He also helped to write the Declaration of Independence.

Ben Franklin was a man of many abilities. He was a businessman, a writer, a scientist, an inventor, and a U.S. diplomat. He wrote a popular magazine called *Poor Richard's Almanac*. It was full of funny sayings, advice, calendars, and information about the weather. He wrote the magazine for twenty-six years.

Ben Franklin was the first American diplomat to France.

Franklin always worked to help his country. He created the first free library in America and the first fire department. In those days, letters were the only way to communicate over long distances. Mail service was not regular or reliable. As the first postmaster general, Ben Franklin created faster routes between the colonies and doubled the speed of mail service. Benjamin Franklin was a man of extraordinary intelligence and energy.

Read the article. Write *GW* for George Washington or *BF* for Ben Franklin.

_____ **1.** He was the leader of the American army.

_____ **2.** He wrote the magazine called Poor Richard's Almanac.

_____ **3.** He is called the Father of Our Country.

_____ **4.** He was the leader of the Constitutional Convention.

_____ **5.** He was older than the other Founding Fathers.

_____ **6.** He was a farmer.

_____ **7.** He started the first free library.

_____ **8.** He was the first President of the United States.

_____ **9.** He was a diplomat for the United States.

_____ **10.** He was the Postmaster General of the United States.

6 READ AND WRITE

A READ. **Go to page 174. Read sentences 9–10 aloud and check your pronunciation.**

B WRITE. **Go to page 176. Listen and write sentences 9–10.**

7 CIVICS IN ACTION

DISCUSS. **Many streets, towns, and cities in the United States are named after famous people in U.S. history. Make a list of streets, towns, or cities you know named after Washington.**

Connect to Your Active Book

Use e-flashcards to prepare for the civics test.

Do the record-and-compare exercises to prepare for the reading test.

Do the writing dictation exercises to prepare for the writing test.

Can you...answer the questions on page 19 about George Washington and Ben Franklin? ☐

LESSON 1 THE UNITED STATES EXPANDS

1 GET READY

A T012 🔊 **Listen to the questions. Do you know the answers?**

- What territory did the United States buy from France in 1803? (Question 71)
- Name <u>one</u> war fought by the United States in the 1800s. (Question 72)

B If you want to check your answers, go to page 205.

2 WHAT DO YOU KNOW?

Look at the map. Which countries controlled the different areas before they became part of the United States of America?

France	Great Britain	Mexico	Spain

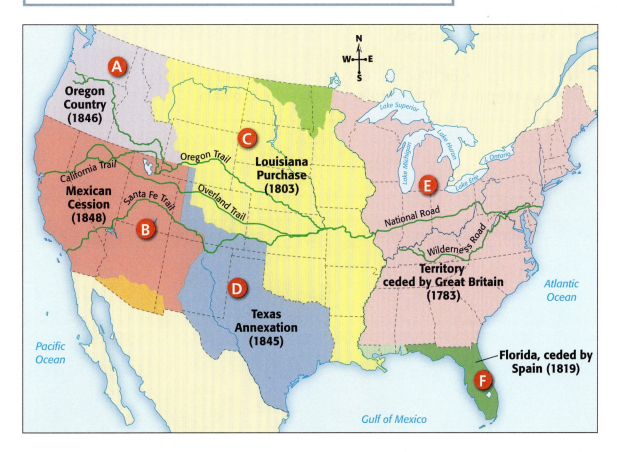

A   **Read the sentences. Do you know the words in bold?**

1. In the 1800s, the United States **expanded** into one of the largest countries in the world.

2. Maine, New Hampshire, and Vermont are on the **border** with Canada.

3. Hawaii was a U.S. **territory** before it became a state.

4. The United States made **agreements** with France, England, and Spain to get more land.

5. In the 1800s, the United States had a large animal skin **trade** with Europe.

6. The United States became an **international** power by 1900.

B   **Match the words and the definitions.**

_____ 1. agreement   **a.** the line between two states or countries

_____ 2. expand   **b.** land ruled by a government

_____ 3. border   **c.** a plan or decision people make together

_____ 4. territory   **d.** involving more than one country

_____ 5. trade   **e.** to become bigger

_____ 6. international   **f.** the buying or selling of things

4   **READ**

A   **T013**   ◀))   **Listen and read the article.**

B   **Read the article again. What land did the U.S. government get through war? Through agreements? Write the places in the correct column.**

Alaska	California	Cuba	Florida	Guam
Hawaii	Louisiana	Nevada	Oregon	Puerto Rico
the Philippines	Utah	Washington		

Land Through Agreements	Land Through Wars
Alaska	

The United States Expands

The United States grew in size during the 1800s. Much of the new land was admitted to the Union as territories. A territory is a region that does not have the same rights and privileges as a state.

From Ocean to Ocean

First, the United States expanded to the west and south. In 1803, the United States bought land, called the Louisiana Purchase, from France for $15 million. Then in 1819, the United States bought Florida from Spain for $5 million.

In 1846, Great Britain gave its northwest territory—what is now the states of Oregon and Washington—to the United States. By 1848, the borders of the United States went from the Atlantic Ocean to the Pacific Ocean. In the late 1800s, the United States expanded beyond these borders. The United States bought Alaska from Russia and took Hawaii as a territory, too.

Settlers moved west across America in covered wagons.

The War of 1812

In the early 1800s, British boats stopped U.S. boats in the Atlantic Ocean. They wanted to stop its trade with other European countries. The young United States wanted to make clear to the world that it was not going to let other countries control its trade. So, the United States went to war against Great Britain in the War of 1812. This war ended in 1815, when both countries signed an agreement to stop fighting.

The Mexican-American War

The United States also won land through war. In 1845, the United States took control of Texas. It became the twenty-eighth state of the nation. This action started the Mexican-American War in 1846. The United States won that war in 1848. Mexico had to give California, Nevada, Utah, and parts of Arizona, Colorado, New Mexico, and Wyoming to the United States.

The Civil War

Although the United States expanded a lot during the 1800s, it was not strong inside its borders. From 1861 to 1865, Americans from the South fought against Americans from the North in the Civil War. More Americans died in this war than in all the other U.S. wars combined.

The Spanish-American War

In 1898, the United States fought Spain in a four-month-long war. It was called the Spanish-American War. The United States won the war and won the Spanish colonies of Cuba and Puerto Rico in the Caribbean, and Guam and the Philippines in the South Pacific. By the end of the Spanish-American War, the United States was a world power.

Culture Note

Today there are fourteen territories still under U.S. control including American Samoa, Guam, the Northern Mariana Islands, Puerto Rico, the U.S. Virgin Islands, and the Minor Outlying Islands.

Read the article. Write the missing information to complete the chart.

Name of War	Involved	Years
		1812–1815
	U.S. and Mexico	
the Civil War		
		1898

A READ. Go to page 174. Read sentences 11–12 aloud and check your pronunciation.

B WRITE. Go to page 176. Listen and write sentences 11–12.

DISCUSS. Find your state on the map on page 23. Which territory was it a part of? Was your state one of the thirteen original states?

Connect to Your Active Book

Use e-flashcards to prepare for the civics test.

Do the record-and-compare exercises to prepare for the reading test.

Do the writing dictation exercises to prepare for the writing test.

Can you...answer the questions on page 23 about the United States in the 1800s? ☐

1   GET READY

A T014 🔊) **Listen to the questions. Do you know the answers?**

- What group of people was taken to America and sold as slaves? (Question 60)
- Name the U.S. war between the North and the South. (Question 73)
- Name <u>one</u> problem that led to the Civil War. (Question 74)

B **If you want to check your answers, go to pages 204 and 205.**

2   WHAT DO YOU KNOW?

Look at the pictures. Who are the people? What is happening?

A Read the sentences. Do you know the words in bold?

1. The farmers **depended** on their slaves to do most of the hard work.
2. Businesses built **factories** along rivers to make cloth.
3. Europeans took Africans from their homes and sold them as **slaves** in America.
4. **Slavery** was a big business between 1600 and 1860.
5. The **economy** of the North grew quickly because of machines.
6. The nation **separated** into two parts: the North and the South.

B Match the words and the definitions.

_____ 1. depend on   **a.** the business of buying and selling people

_____ 2. factory   **b.** to need somebody or something

_____ 3. slave   **c.** the way a country spends its money, and makes, buys, and sell things

_____ 4. slavery   **d.** to break and divide up into parts

_____ 5. economy   **e.** a person who belongs to someone else and works for free

_____ 6. separate   **f.** a place where people make things to sell

4 **READ**

A T015 🔊 Listen and read the article.

B Read the article again. Then complete the sentences. Write *North* or *South.*

1. The _____ wanted to separate from the United States.
2. The _____ was also called the Confederacy.
3. The _____ had small farms and many factories.
4. The _____ wanted to protect its states' rights.
5. The _____ did not have as many slaves.
6. The _____ had large farms.
7. The _____ had many slaves.
8. The _____ wanted the country to be united.
9. The _____ wanted to change the slavery laws in the South.
10. The _____ won the Civil War.
11. The _____ lost the Civil War.

The War Between the North and South

Slavery

From the 1500s to the 1800s, people were taken from their homes in Africa and sold as slaves in America. They were brought over on crowded ships. Many died on the way. The slaves had no control over their lives. They had no human rights. The slaves worked long hours for no pay. Their owners could buy and sell them whenever they wanted. Husbands were separated from wives, and children were separated from parents.

Some people in the United States disagreed with slavery. They said it was against a person's right to liberty, which is a right in the U.S. Constitution.

Economic Reasons

The Southern states depended on slavery for economic reasons. States such as Virginia and South Carolina had very large farms. They grew tobacco and cotton. They depended on the free work of slaves. Slavery was a part of the economy and life of the South.

The Northern states had a very different economy. They had small family farms, which did not need slaves. They had large cities with factories. Slavery was not a big part of the Northern economy. By the 1850s, slavery was against the law in most Northern states.

States' Rights

More and more people in the North wanted slavery to end. But the Southern states had laws to support slavery. The Southern states said the federal government had no right to change their laws. They had states' rights.

The War between the States

Between 1860 and 1861, eleven Southern states decided to leave the United States and become a separate nation. They called it the Confederacy. The President of the United States, Abraham Lincoln, wanted to keep the country together. He would not let the Southern states leave without a fight.

For the next four years the North and South fought each other in the Civil War, also known as the War between the States. In 1865, the war ended. The North won the Civil War and the United States became one nation again.

Culture Note

During the American Civil War (1861–1865), people from the North were called Yankees, and people from the South were called Confederates. Confederates were also known as Rebels.

Free states
Slave states

By the 1850s, slavery was only in the South.

Read the article. Write *T* for True or *F* for False. Then correct the false sentences.

_____ 1. George Washington was President of the United States during the Civil War.

_____ 2. States' rights mean that states have the right to make their own laws.

_____ 3. Many people thought that slaves did not have human rights.

_____ 4. The economies of the North and the South were the same.

_____ 5. People from Africa were taken to America and sold as slaves.

_____ 6. The war between the North and the South was called the Civil War.

_____ 7. The Northern states wanted laws to support slavery.

_____ 8. The Civil War is also called the Confederacy.

_____ 9. Large factories in the North depended on the free work of slaves.

6   READ AND WRITE

A READ. **Go to page 174. Read sentences 13–14 aloud and check your pronunciation.**

B WRITE. **Go to page 176. Listen and write sentences 13–14.**

7   CIVICS IN ACTION

DISCUSS. **Do you think there is equality in the United States today? Why or why not? Give examples.**

Connect to Your Active Book

Use e-flashcards to prepare for the civics test.

Do the record-and-compare exercises to prepare for the reading test.

Do the writing dictation exercises to prepare for the writing test.

Can you...answer the questions on page 27 about slavery and the Civil War? ☐

LESSON 3 ABRAHAM LINCOLN

1 GET READY

A 🔊 **T016** **Listen to the questions. Do you know the answers?**

- What was <u>one</u> important thing that Abraham Lincoln did? (Question 75)
- What did the Emancipation Proclamation do? (Question 76)

B **If you want to check your answers, go to page 205.**

2 WHAT DO YOU KNOW?

Look at the pictures. Why is Abraham Lincoln important?

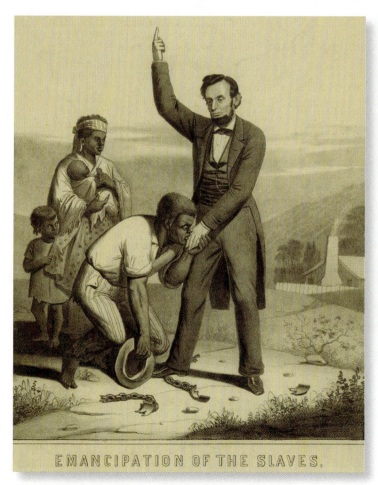

EMANCIPATION OF THE SLAVES,

Abraham Lincoln signed the Emancipation Proclamation in 1863.

The Lincoln Memorial is in Washington, D.C.

Do you know the words in bold? What do the sentences mean? Circle _a_ or _b_.

1. The Civil War **destroyed** many farms and roads in the South.
   a. After the war, the farms and roads were busy.
   b. After the war, many farms and roads were gone.

2. President Lincoln gave great **speeches**. People today still read his words.
   a. He gave interesting talks to groups of people.
   b. He was interested in writing books for people.

3. President Lincoln wanted to **preserve the union** of the United States.
   a. He wanted to create two countries.
   b. He wanted to keep the United States as one country.

4. Since the Civil War, there has been **peace** between the North and the South.
   a. War has continued between the North and the South.
   b. There has been no more war between the North and the South.

5. President Lincoln made the **proclamation** that the slaves were free.
   a. He decided that all slaves were free.
   b. He wished that all slaves were free.

6. President Lincoln wrote an **amendment** to the Constitution to free all slaves in the United States.
   a. He wrote a new U.S. constitution to give freedom to all slaves.
   b. He made a change to the U.S. Constitution to give freedom to all slaves.

4 READ

A T017 🔊 Listen and read the article.

B Read the article again. Then complete the sentences. Use the words in the box.

| Confederacy | Emancipation Proclamation | President |
| Thirteenth Amendment | union | |

1. The Southern states called their new country the _____.

2. Lincoln wanted to save the _____.

3. The _____ freed the slaves in the Confederacy.

4. Abraham Lincoln was _____ during the Civil War.

5. The _____ finally freed all the slaves in the United States.

Abraham Lincoln

Abraham Lincoln was president from 1861 to 1865. He was president during one of the most difficult times in United States history. Abraham Lincoln led the United States during the Civil War.

In 1860, a month before Abraham Lincoln became President, Southern states had already separated from the United States to become the *Confederate States of America*, or the Confederacy. When Lincoln became President, he promised to keep the United States together. He wanted to "preserve the union," and he was ready to fight a war if necessary.

The Emancipation Proclamation

Lincoln also wanted to free the slaves, but he did not want to divide the country even more. Four slave states stayed with the Union. Lincoln worried that these states would turn against the Union if he freed all the slaves immediately. Instead, he went slowly.

In 1863, in the middle of the war, Lincoln signed the Emancipation Proclamation. This proclamation did not free all slaves in the United States, but it did free slaves in the Confederacy. This meant in most Southern states, the slaves were free.

The Thirteenth Amendment

Toward the end of the war, Abraham Lincoln asked the Congress to pass the Thirteenth Amendment to the U.S. Constitution. The amendment passed in 1865 making all the slaves in the United States free.

The Civil War, 1861–1865

Saving the Union

On April 9, 1865, the North won the war. Abraham Lincoln saved the union! But the four-year war had hurt the country, especially the South. More than 3 million Americans fought in the war and more than 600,000 people died. Most of the fighting was in the South. When the war ended, the South was destroyed.

Lincoln was ready to help the South. He wanted the whole country to move quickly beyond the war. In a speech he gave near the end of the war, called the Gettsyburg Address, he asked the American people to take care of anyone who was hurt by the war. He asked Americans to work together toward peace.

Five days after the war ended, President Lincoln was killed by a person who wanted the South to win. President Lincoln saved the union of the United States, but he lost his life because of the Civil War.

5 CHECK YOUR UNDERSTANDING

Read the article. Number the events to put them in time order.

_____ **a.** The Civil War ended.

_____ **b.** Abraham Lincoln became president of the United States.

_____ **c.** President Lincoln was killed.

_____ **d.** The Civil War began.

_____ **e.** President Lincoln signed the Emancipation Proclamation.

_____ **f.** President Lincoln gave the Gettysburg address.

__1__ **g.** Eleven southern states left the United States to become the Confederacy.

6 READ AND WRITE

A **READ.** Go to page 174. Read sentences 15–16 aloud and check your pronunciation.

B **WRITE.** Go to page 176. Listen and write sentences 15–16.

7 CIVICS IN ACTION

DISCUSS. Abraham Lincoln made decisions that greatly affected the future of the United States. Who are leaders in your native country who made decisions that greatly affected your country's history?

Connect to Your Active Book

Use e-flashcards to prepare for the civics test.

Do the record-and-compare exercises to prepare for the reading test.

Do the writing dictation exercises to prepare for the writing test.

Can you... answer the questions on page 31 about Abraham Lincoln? ☐

LESSON 4 EQUAL RIGHTS

1 GET READY

A 🔊 **T018** Listen to the question. Do you know the answer?

• What did Susan B. Anthony do? (Question 77)

B If you want to check your answer, go to page 205.

2 WHAT DO YOU KNOW?

Look at the pictures. Who are the people? What are they doing?

A Read the sentences. Do you know the words in bold?

1. For many years in the United States, slaves and women did not have **civil rights**.
2. Before 1920, women were **citizens** but they could not vote.
3. There was no **equality** between men and women.
4. Women did not have the right to own **property**.
5. Women did not have the **opportunity** to get good jobs.
6. Some people did not think women would be allowed to vote. They thought the fight for women's rights was a **failure**.

B Match the words and the definitions.

_____ 1. citizen
_____ 2. civil rights
_____ 3. equality
_____ 4. failure
_____ 5. opportunity
_____ 6. property

a. something that someone owns
b. a person's right to freedom and equal treatment
c. a chance to do something
d. a person who lives in a country and has rights
e. not having success
f. having the same rights

4 READ

A 🔊 T019 Listen and read the article.

B Read the article again. Then complete the sentences. Write the letter.

_____ 1. Women did not always
_____ 2. Women were citizens of the United States,
_____ 3. White men controlled property
_____ 4. After Susan B. Anthony helped black men get the vote,
_____ 5. Susan gave speeches, organized people,
_____ 6. In 1920, the Nineteenth Amendment

a. she worked on women's right to vote.
b. gave <u>all</u> women the right to vote.
c. have equal rights in the United States.
d. and fought for civil rights and human rights.
e. but they did not have the right to vote.
f. and had the right to vote.

Susan B. Anthony

The Fight for Women's Rights

Women did not always have equal rights in the United States. For many years, they did not have the right to control their property or the right to vote. Women had to fight for their rights. One of these women was Susan B. Anthony.

Susan B. Anthony was born in 1820 in New England. Her family believed in the equal rights of all people and in the importance of education. Susan's parents made sure Susan received an education equal to her brothers'. At the time, this was unusual. Most families didn't think women needed much education.

Susan B. Anthony grew up when only white men had the right to vote. Black men and women and white women could not vote. Susan realized that many people in the world did not believe in civil rights. She decided to use her energy and education to make changes.

The Fight for Civil Rights

Before and during the Civil War, Susan B. Anthony fought to end slavery. After the war, when black men were given the right to vote, she worked on a woman's right to vote. She traveled the country, gave speeches, wrote books and magazines, and organized people to speak out. Susan B. Anthony fought for civil rights.

The Nineteenth Amendment

Susan B. Anthony talked about the ideas of equality in the U.S. Constitution. Women were citizens of the United States, but they did not have the right to vote. Near the end of Susan B. Anthony's life, women had better opportunities, but only four states gave women the right to vote.

Right before Susan B. Anthony died, she said, "Failure is impossible." Finally, in 1920, fourteen years after her death, the Nineteenth Amendment to the U.S. Constitution gave all women the right to vote. It is called the *Susan B. Anthony Amendment*.

The Susan B. Anthony dollar

5 CHECK YOUR UNDERSTANDING

Read the article. Write *T* for True or *F* for False. Then correct the false sentences.

_____ 1. Susan B. Anthony had a good education.

_____ 2. Susan B. Anthony believed men and women should have equal rights.

_____ 3. Women always had equal rights in the United States.

_____ 4. Susan B. Anthony died before women had the right to vote.

_____ 5. In the United States, black men had the right to vote before black women.

_____ 6. Susan B. Anthony fought for civil rights and men's rights.

_____ 7. In the United States, women got the right to vote in 1914.

_____ 8. The Thirteenth Amendment gave all women the right to vote.

6 READ AND WRITE

A READ. Go to page 174. Read sentences 17–18 aloud and check your pronunciation.

B WRITE. Go to page 176. Listen and write sentences 17–18.

7 CIVICS IN ACTION

DISCUSS. How are women involved in politics and political decisions in your community? In your city? In your state?

Connect to Your Active Book

Use e-flashcards to prepare for the civics test.

Do the record-and-compare exercises to prepare for the reading test.

Do the writing dictation exercises to prepare for the writing test.

Can you... answer the question on page 35 about Susan B. Anthony? ☐

LESSON 1   WORLD WARS I AND II

1   GET READY

T020

A 🔊 **Listen to the questions. Do you know the answers?**

- Who was President during World War I? (Question 79)
- Who was President during the Great Depression and World War II? (Question 80)
- Who did the United States fight in World War II? (Question 81)
- Before he was President, Eisenhower was a general. What war was he in? (Question 82)

B **If you want to check your answers, go to page 205.**

2   WHAT DO YOU KNOW?

Look at the pictures. Who are these U.S. presidents?
Label the pictures. Use the names in the box.

Dwight D. Eisenhower	Franklin D. Roosevelt	Woodrow Wilson

1. _____   2. _____   3. _____

A Read the sentences. Do you know the words in bold?

1. The United States fought in six wars in the 20th **century**.

2. Many different **ethnic** groups lived in Europe in the 1900s.

3. People made a lot of money in the **stock market** in the 1920s.

4. The United States **joined** England, France, and the Soviet Union in World War II.

5. Dwight Eisenhower was a **hero** in World War II.

6. In World War II, Germany **invaded** many countries in Europe, including France, Poland, Hungary, and Belgium.

B Match the words and the definitions.

_____ **1.** century   **a.** a particular race, nationality, or group of people

_____ **2.** ethnic   **b.** to come together with other people or groups

_____ **3.** stock market   **c.** to go into another country to control it

_____ **4.** join   **d.** a person who has done something good and brave

_____ **5.** hero   **e.** a period of 100 years

_____ **6.** invade   **f.** a place where people buy and sell shares in businesses

4 **READ**

A T021 🔊 Listen and read the article.

B Read the article again. Then complete the sentences. Use the words in the box.

Eisenhower	Germany	Roosevelt
the United States	World War I	World War II

1. Wilson was President of the United States during _____.

2. _____ was President during the Great Depression.

3. _____, Japan, and Italy fought _____ in World War II.

4. Roosevelt was President of the United States during _____.

5. _____ was a general in World War II.

Struggles at Home and Away

The United States went through many changes in the first half of the twentieth century. At the beginning of the century, the United States was a large, but not so important country. By the time World War II ended, it was the most powerful country in the world.

World War I

World War I began in 1914. It began between European countries, but soon it involved many of the European colonies in Asia and Africa, too. Woodrow Wilson was President of the United States during World War I. Wilson tried to keep the United States out of the war, but in 1917, it decided to join the fight. World War I ended in 1918, but it was not a very secure peace.

The Great Depression

In the 1920s, the economy in the United States grew quickly. People made a lot of money in businesses and in the stock market, but in 1929 the good times ended. The U.S. stock market crashed. Many banks lost their money and closed. People lost their jobs and their homes. This period of time was called the Great Depression. It ended in the late 1930s.

Franklin D. Roosevelt was president during the Great Depression. He created many government programs to help people survive those very hard years. In 1935, he created the Social Security Administration and unemployment insurance. Roosevelt also put people to work building bridges, roads, and buildings. He called his plan the New Deal.

World War II

In 1933, Adolph Hitler came to power in Germany. He believed that some of the German people were better than other people. He wanted to kill other ethnic groups in Europe, especially the Jews. Hitler wanted to create a German empire, so he invaded many countries.

World War II began in 1939. Roosevelt did not want to get involved in the big war in Europe. But then Japan and Italy joined Germany. On December 7, 1941, Japan attacked U.S. ships in Pearl Harbor, Hawaii. The United States declared war the next day. The United States joined Britain, France, and the Soviet Union in the fight against Germany, Japan, and Italy. World War II ended in 1944. About 60 million people died around the world because of this terrible war.

The first half of the 1900s was a time of tremendous difficulty and change. It was also a time when the United States became an international power.

CHECK YOUR UNDERSTANDING

Read the article. Number the events to put them in time order.

World War I

_____ **a.** The United States joined World War I.

_____ **b.** World War I began.

_____ **c.** European colonies joined World War I.

World War II

_____ **a.** World War II began.

_____ **b.** Hitler came to power.

_____ **c.** Japan bombed Hawaii.

_____ **d.** The United States joined England, France, and the Soviet Union.

The Great Depression

_____ **a.** In the early 1920s, people made a lot of money.

_____ **b.** The Great Depression ended.

_____ **c.** Roosevelt created the Social Security Administration and unemployment insurance.

_____ **d.** The stock market crashed.

6 READ AND WRITE

A **READ.** Go to page 174. Read sentences 19–20 aloud and check your pronunciation.

B **WRITE.** Go to page 176. Listen and write sentences 19–20.

7 CIVICS IN ACTION

DISCUSS. Think of a war in your native country or in another country. Why did it happen? What changed because of the war?

Connect to Your Active Book

Use e-flashcards to prepare for the civics test.

Do the record-and-compare exercises to prepare for the reading test.

Do the writing dictation exercises to prepare for the writing test.

Can you... answer the questions on page 39 about World Wars I and II? ☐

Lesson 2 20th Century Wars

1 GET READY

T022

A 🔊)) **Listen to the questions. Do you know the answers?**

- What is the economic system in the United States? (Question 11)
- Name <u>one</u> war fought by the United States in the 1900s. (Question 78)
- During the Cold War, what was the main concern of the United States? (Question 83)

B **If you want to check your answers, go to pages 202 and 205.**

2 WHAT DO YOU KNOW?

Look at the map. Point to the countries listed in the box.

China	Cuba	Iraq	Kuwait	North Korea
Russia	the U.S.	Venezuela	Vietnam	

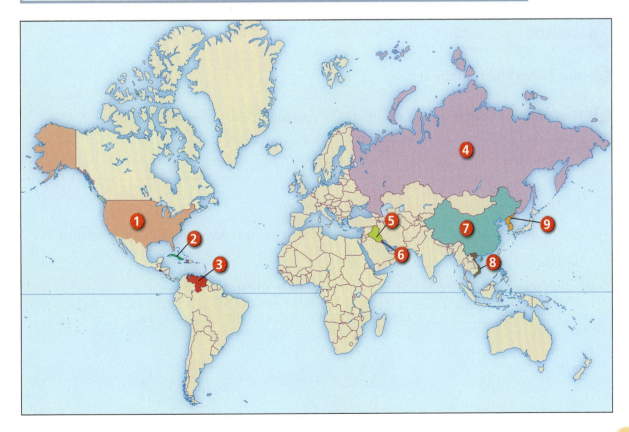

BEFORE YOU READ

A Read the sentences. Do you know the words in bold?

1. The **economic systems** of the United States and the Soviet Union were very different.

2. The Soviet Union had a system of **communism**.

3. The United States has a **market economy**.

4. The **main concern** of the United States was the expansion of communism.

5. The United States **got involved** in many wars to stop communism.

6. In the end, the people of the Soviet Union **tore down** the wall that separated them from the market economy.

B Match the words and the definitions.

_____ 1. economic system

_____ 2. communism

_____ 3. market economy

_____ 4. main concern

_____ 5. get involved

_____ 6. tear down

a. to destroy

b. people share everything; no one has more money than another person

c. the most important problem

d. people make their own money; some people have more money and some people have less

e. the way a country uses its money and buys and sells goods

f. to participate

4 **READ**

A T023 🔊 Listen and read the article.

B Read the article again. Then complete the sentences. Use the words in the box.

Cold War	Gulf War	Korean War	United States	Vietnam War

1. The _____ has a market economy.

2. During the _____, the United States was concerned about communism.

3. The United States fought in both the _____ and the _____ because it was concerned about communism in the two countries.

4. The _____ involved Iraq, Kuwait, and the United States.

100 Years of War

In the 1900s, the United States fought in five wars: World War I, World War II, the Korean War, the Vietnam War, and the Persian Gulf War. In the 100 years between 1900 and 2000, the United States became a world power.

At the beginning of the 1900s, the United States didn't want to get involved in world politics. It was slow to get involved in World Wars I and II. But after World War II, the United States was stronger than other countries. The United States played a role in the Korean, Vietnam, and Persian Gulf Wars because it had become an international power.

The Cold War

In the 1950s, the United States got involved in a new kind of war. It was a war of ideas. It was called the Cold War. The economic system of the United States is a capitalist economy, also called a market economy. This means that people have private property. They own businesses and make their own money. In the 1950s, the Soviet Union also became a world power. In the Soviet economy, people did not have private property. The government owned all property and shared it with the people. Communism was the main concern of the United States during the Cold War.

Culture Note

After World War II, Berlin in Germany was divided. The Berlin Wall separated families and neighborhoods. East Berlin was communist. West Berlin was a market economy. The Berlin Wall became the symbol of the Cold War. In 1987, President Reagan made a speech in Berlin and said, "Tear down this wall." Two years later, in 1989, the wall came down.

After World War II, the Soviet Union had communist control of Eastern Europe. Then China became communist. Other countries, such as Cuba, Chile, Venezuela, and Vietnam, started to follow communist thinking. The United States was worried more countries would become communist. The United States got involved in the wars in Korea (1950–1953) and Vietnam (1959–1975) because it didn't want these countries to become communist.

By the end of the 1980s, the Soviet system began to fall apart. By 1991, most Soviet communist countries returned to market economies. The Cold War was over.

The Persian Gulf War

As the Cold War ended, a new war began. The Persian Gulf War started in 1990. Iraq invaded the small country of Kuwait. The United States got involved in the war against Iraq in January 1991. By the end of February, the war was over and Kuwait was independent again.

U.S. troops during the Persian Gulf War

5 CHECK YOUR UNDERSTANDING

Read the article. When did the wars take place? Write each war on the timeline.

the Persian Gulf War	the Korean War	the Vietnam War
World War I	World War II	

1914–1918   1939–1945   1950–1953   1959–1975   1990–1991

6 READ AND WRITE

A READ. Go to page 174. Read sentences 21–22 aloud and check your pronunciation.

B WRITE. Go to page 176. Listen and write sentences 21–22.

7 CIVICS IN ACTION

DISCUSS. Veterans are men and women who have served in the military. Are there any veteran organizations in your community? What kinds of services do they offer?

Connect to Your Active Book

Use e-flashcards to prepare for the civics test.

Do the record-and-compare exercises to prepare for the reading test.

Do the writing dictation exercises to prepare for the writing test.

Can you...answer the questions on page 43 about wars during the 20th century? ☐

LESSON 3 THE CIVIL RIGHTS MOVEMENT

1   GET READY

A T024 🔊 **Listen to the questions. Do you know the answers?**

- What movement tried to end racial discrimination? (Question 84)
- What did Martin Luther King, Jr. do? (Question 85)

B **If you want to check your answers, go to page 205.**

2   WHAT DO YOU KNOW?

Look at the pictures. Who is the man? What do you know about him?

Do you know the words in bold? What do the sentences mean? Circle *a* or *b*.

1. Slavery has a **violent** history.
   a. Slaves were treated badly.
   b. Slaves were treated well.

2. There has been **racial discrimination** in the United States.
   a. African Americans have been treated differently because of the color of their skin.
   b. African Americans and white people have been treated the same way.

3. Martin Luther King, Jr. **protested** the way African Americans were treated.
   a. He accepted the way African Americans were treated.
   b. He spoke out against the way African Americans were treated.

4. Many people were **arrested** in the 1950s and 1960s.
   a. People were taken by the police and put in jail.
   b. People were on the TV and radio.

5. Many people **boycotted** businesses that were unfair to blacks.
   a. People didn't walk to the businesses.
   b. People didn't shop at the businesses.

6. In the 1900s there were several important **movements** for change.
   a. People talking to each other to change laws.
   b. People working together to change laws.

4 **READ**

A T025 🔊 **Listen and read the article.**

B **Read the article again. Then complete the sentences. Use the words in the box.**

civil rights movement	discrimination	equal rights
peaceful	Rosa Parks	

1. There was _____ against blacks in schools and government.

2. The _____ tried to end racial discrimination.

3. Martin Luther King, Jr. worked for _____ for all Americans.

4. Martin Luther King, Jr. told people to have _____ protests.

5. _____ was arrested on a bus.

I Have a Dream

Slavery ended in the United States in 1865, but racial discrimination continued. Blacks lived with discrimination in every part of their lives: while working, shopping, traveling, and voting. The civil rights movement tried to end racial discrimination.

Separate and Unequal

During the early part of the 1900s, many states in the South passed laws to separate white and black people. African Americans could not go to the same schools as whites. They could not go through the same front doors or drink from the same water fountain. In some states, African Americans could not even vote. They had to pass a test to be able to vote. White people did not have to take the test. Blacks lived in a separate and unequal world.

Laws separated white people from "colored" people.

Rosa Parks

In the 1940s and '50s in Alabama only whites could sit in the front of a bus. That was the law. Black people had to sit in the back. When there were no more front seats for the whites, the blacks had to give up their seats and stand.

Culture Note

On August 28, 1963, Dr. Martin Luther King, Jr. led a civil rights protest to the Lincoln Memorial in Washington, D.C. King gave his most famous speech, "I Have a Dream." He talked about his hope that all people, black and white, would be known for their abilities and not by the color of their skin.

On December 1, 1955, Rosa Parks, a forty-one-year-old African-American woman, got on a bus in Montgomery, Alabama. She was tired after a long day of work. She sat down behind the white people, but it was in the middle of the bus. Soon the bus driver told her to stand up so a white man could take her seat. She said, "No." Rosa Parks was arrested.

Rosa Parks

Martin Luther King, Jr.

Many people were angry when Rosa Parks was arrested. They asked a church leader, Dr. Martin Luther King, Jr., to organize a protest. He wanted a peaceful protest. He said it was not possible to change history with violence.

Dr. King and his group decided to boycott the buses. They stopped taking the city buses. Instead the African Americans in Montgomery, Alabama walked. They walked to work, and they walked to stores. They also shared their cars.

The boycott was hard, but it worked. After 381 days, the Supreme Court decided that the bus laws in Alabama were not constitutional. It was against the U.S. Constitution to separate whites and blacks on buses. Dr. King won his first fight.

The Civil Rights Movement

Dr. King continued to fight for civil rights and work for equality for all Americans. In 1964, the Civil Rights Act was passed. Ever since, it has been against the law to discriminate against people because of the color of their skin.

Read the article. Complete the sentences. Circle *a* or *b*.

1. There was _____ blacks until the laws changed in the 1960s.
   a. equality for
   b. discrimination against

2. _____ tried to end racial discrimination
   a. The Civil Rights Movement
   b. The Southern states

3. Dr. Martin Luther King, Jr. worked for _____.
   a. the U.S. government
   b. equality for all Americans

4. Rosa Parks was arrested because she _____ her bus seat to a white man.
   a. gave
   b. didn't give

5. Martin Luther King's most famous speech is called _____.
   a. "I Have a Dream"
   b. "The Lincoln Memorial"

6. Dr. King wanted to have _____ protests.
   a. violent
   b. peaceful

6   READ AND WRITE

A READ. Go to page 174. Read sentences 23–24 aloud and check your pronunciation.

B WRITE. Go to page 176. Listen and write sentences 23–24.

7   CIVICS IN ACTION

DISCUSS. What boycotts do you know about in your community? In the United States? In your native country? Describe the reasons for the boycott.

Connect to Your Active Book

Use e-flashcards to prepare for the civics test.

Do the record-and-compare exercises to prepare for the reading test.

Do the writing dictation exercises to prepare for the writing test.

Can you...answer the questions on page 47 about the Civil Rights Movement? ☐

LESSON 4 SEPTEMBER 11, 2001

1 GET READY

A T026 🔊 **Listen to the question. Do you know the answer?**

- What major event happened on September 11, 2001, in the United States? (Question 86)

B **If you want to check your answer, go to page 205.**

2 WHAT DO YOU KNOW?

Look at the map. Do you know what happened at each location?

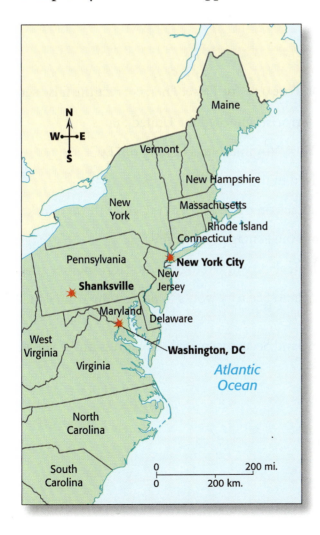

Complete the definitions. Use the words in the box.

crash	event	hijack
military	security	terrorist

1. _____: someone who hurts or kills others to make people or the government do what he/she wants

2. _____: to take control of a plane and fly it to a different place

3. _____: to move fast toward something and hit it hard

4. _____: an important thing that happens

5. _____: means safety and protection

6. _____: anything connected with soldiers, armies, or war

4 READ

A T027 🔊) **Listen and read the article.**

B Read the article again. Write *T* for True or *F* for False. Then correct the false sentences.

_____ **1.** On September 11, 2001, terrorists attacked the United States.

_____ **2.** Terrorists attacked New York, Virginia, and Washington, D.C.

_____ **3.** Two airplanes were involved in the attack.

_____ **4.** Most people died in the attack on the World Trade Center in New York City.

_____ **5.** Two airplanes crashed into the Pentagon in Virginia.

_____ **6.** The people on the fourth airplane worked together to stop another attack.

_____ **7.** The Department of Homeland Security works to protect the United States from terrorist attacks.

_____ **8.** The Department of Homeland Security created the expression "If you see something, say something."

America under Attack

On September 11, 2001, terrorists attacked the United States. Terrorists hijacked four airplanes. They flew two of the airplanes into the Twin Towers of the World Trade Center in New York City. The crashes started a terrible fire. Within two hours, the two tall buildings fell to the ground. Thousands of people died.

The third airplane flew into the Pentagon in Arlington, Virginia. The Pentagon is the center for U.S. military offices. It is very close to Washington, D.C. More than 100 people died in that attack.

The fourth airplane was flying to San Francisco. It was hijacked by terrorists and turned around to fly to Washington, D.C. The passengers on the airplane were talking to family and friends on their cell phones. They heard about the other crashes. They realized they were part of a terrorist plan. They took control of the plane from the hijackers. They decided to crash the plane to stop the terrorists' plan. They crashed the airplane into a field in Pennsylvania. Everyone on the airplane died.

The events on September 11, 2001, changed the United States in many ways. The U.S. government created a new office. It is called the *Department of Homeland Security*. It works to protect people and respond to emergencies in the United States, especially terrorist attacks. "If you see something, say something" was a slogan used by New York City after the attacks of 9/11. New York City wanted everyone to help keep the city safe.

The government is now also very careful about who enters the country. Citizen and Immigration Services is part of the Department of Homeland Security. New security rules are everywhere: at borders, in airports, and on public transportation.

A passenger going through airport security

Firefighters raised the American flag after 9/11.

A Think about the events of 9/11. Write sentences describing what happened. Use the words in the box.

a field	crash/crashed	Homeland Security	New York City
passengers	Pennsylvania	the Pentagon	planes
September 11	terrorist attacks	Twin Towers	Virginia

_____

_____

_____

_____

_____

B Find a partner. Talk about the events of 9/11. Use your sentences in Exercise A.

6 READ AND WRITE

A READ. Go to page 174. Read sentences 25–26 aloud and check your pronunciation.

B WRITE. Go to page 176. Listen and write sentences 25–26.

7 CIVICS IN ACTION

DISCUSS. What are some of the new security regulations after September 11, 2001? Have they affected you? How?

Connect to Your Active Book

Use e-flashcards to prepare for the civics test.

Do the record-and-compare exercises to prepare for the reading test.

Do the writing dictation exercises to prepare for the writing test.

Can you...answer the question on page 51 about September 11, 2001? ☐

Lesson 1 The Constitution

1 GET READY

A T028 🔊 Listen to the questions. Do you know the answers?

- What is the supreme law of the land? (Question 1)
- What does the Constitution do? (Question 2)
- The idea of self-government is in the first three words of the Constitution. What are these words? (Question 3)
- What is an amendment? (Question 4)
- How many amendments does the Constitution have? (Question 7)
- What is the "rule of law"? (Question 12)

B If you want to check your answers, go to page 202.

2 WHAT DO YOU KNOW?

Look at the Constitution of the United States. What are the first three words? Why do you think these words are important to Americans?

Do you know the words in bold? What do they mean? Circle *a* or *b*.

1. The Constitution is **the supreme law of the land**.
   a. the most important law in the U.S.   b. the oldest law in the U.S.

2. Everyone in the United States must **obey** the laws.
   a. do what they say   b. agree with what they say

3. The President is the **leader** of the United States.
   a. the person at the top   b. the second in command

4. The U.S. government has three **branches**: the executive branch, the judicial branch, and the legislative branch.
   a. laws   b. parts

5. The Constitution **defines the government**.
   a. is against the government   b. explains what the government is

4 READ

A T029 🔊)) **Listen and read the article.**

B **Read the article again. Answer the questions. Circle *a* or *b*.**

1. What does the Constitution do?
   a. It organizes the U.S. government.   b. It follows the laws.

2. How many amendments does the U.S. Constitution have?
   a. ten   b. twenty-seven

3. What does the rule of law mean?
   a. No one is above the law.   b. Everyone is above the law.

4. What is an amendment?
   a. a new Constitution   b. an addition to the Constitution

5. Who wrote the U.S. Constitution?
   a. The Founding Fathers   b. We the people

6. Who runs the government?
   a. The Founding Fathers   b. We the people

7. What are the first ten amendments called?
   a. The Articles of the Constitution   b. The Bill of Rights

The Supreme Law of the Land

Culture Note

On December 7, 1787, Delaware became the first of the original 13 states to approve the new Constitution.

The United States Constitution is the supreme law of the land. No law is higher than the Constitution in the United States. The Constitution was written in 1787 by the Founding Fathers. It defines the government and protects the basic rights of all Americans. The Constitution is divided into three parts: the Preamble, the Articles of the Constitution, and the Amendments.

Preamble

The first three words of the Constitution are *We the people*. This means the country is run by the people. It explains the idea of self-government. If the people do not like what the government is doing, they can change the government. The government works for the people.

Articles of the Constitution

This part of the Constitution organizes the government. Article I defines the legislative branch, the part of the government that makes laws. Article II defines the executive branch, which includes the positions of President and Vice President. Article III defines the judicial branch, the part of government that explains the laws. Each branch has specific responsibilities.

Amendments

The writers of the Constitution knew that over time people would need to make small changes to the Constitution. A change or addition to the Constitution is an amendment. The Founding Fathers set up a special part of the Constitution for amendments. Now there are twenty-seven amendments to the Constitution. The first ten amendments are called The Bill of Rights. These amendments were written to protect the basic rights of everyone in the United States.

The Rule of Law

The Founding Fathers wrote the U.S. Constitution because they believed in the rule of law. They believed no one is above the law. Everyone must follow the law. Leaders must obey the law. The government must obey the law. The President, the members of Congress, and the Justices of the Supreme Court all must follow the rule of law.

Read the article. Then complete the sentences. Use the words in the box.

amendment	Bill of Rights	Constitution	self-government
the Founding Fathers	the rule of law	We the people	

1. The supreme law of the land is the _____.

2. The first ten amendments to the Constitution are called the _____.

3. The first three words of the U.S. Constitution are _____.

4. The U.S. Constitution was written by _____.

5. _____ says that everyone must follow the law.

6. A change to the U.S. Constitution is called an _____.

7. The power to govern that comes from the people is called _____.

6 READ AND WRITE

A READ. Go to page 174. Read sentences 27–28 aloud and check your pronunciation.

B WRITE. Go to page 176. Listen and write sentences 27–28.

7 CIVICS IN ACTION

DISCUSS. What kind of document describes the laws of your country?
How is it similar to or different than the U.S. Constitution?

Connect to Your Active Book

Use e-flashcards to prepare for the civics test.

Do the record-and-compare exercises to prepare for the reading test.

Do the writing dictation exercises to prepare for the writing test.

Can you…answer the questions on page 55 about the U.S. Constitution? ☐

1 GET READY

A T030 🔊)) **Listen to the questions. Do you know the answers?**

- What do we call the first ten amendments to the Constitution? (Question 5)
- What is <u>one</u> right or freedom from the First Amendment? (Question 6)
- What is freedom of religion? (Question 10)

B **If you want to check your answers, go to page 202.**

2 WHAT DO YOU KNOW?

Look at the pictures. Who are the people? What are they doing?

Complete the definitions. Use the words in the box.

assembly	crime	jury	lawyer	petition	the press	trial

1. _____: includes newspapers, TV, and the Internet

2. _____: an action that is against the law

3. _____: the group of people in a court who decide if a person has done something against the law

4. _____: a person who studies law and represents people in court

5. _____: the process of hearing and judging a person in a court

6. _____: when people meet together for a special purpose

7. _____: a letter to the government asking for change and signed by many people

4 READ

A 🔊 **Listen and read the article.**
T031

B **Read the article again. Which right or freedom is protected in each situation?**

Situation 1

A newspaper finds out the mayor of a city accepted money from a businessperson. The newspaper writes articles to explain what happened. The mayor gets arrested. The newspaper is protected by the freedom of _____.

Situation 2

There's a new tax on restaurants. You own a restaurant. You don't agree with the law. You write a letter to your representative. You explain why you don't like the law. You are protected by the freedom of _____ and the freedom to petition the government.

Situation 3

You think the government should have better laws to protect workers and to create more jobs. You go to Washington, D.C. with thousands of other people to protest. You are protected by the freedom of speech and the freedom of _____.

Situation 4

The country is at war. The government wants all men between eighteen and twenty-five years of age to fight. It is against your family's religion to kill. The government says your son can do a different kind of service for the nation. Your son is protected by the freedom of _____.

Rights for Everyone

The first ten amendments to the Constitution are called the Bill of Rights. The Founding Fathers added these amendments to make sure everyone's rights were protected from a powerful government. The First Amendment protects many basic rights of people in the United States.

Freedom of Speech

The First Amendment protects the freedom of speech. This means people can say what they believe. They can disagree with the government. They cannot be arrested for what they say or think.

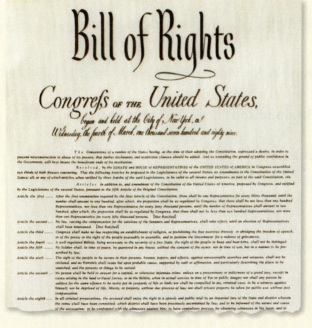

Freedom of Religion

The First Amendment protects our freedom of religion. This means we can practice any religion, or not practice religion at all. We are free to choose.

Freedom of Assembly

The First Amendment protects the freedom of assembly. We are free to have meetings in public, such as in parks, schools, and government centers. We are free to protest against the government.

Freedom of the Press

The First Amendment protects the freedom of the press. Newspapers, magazines, books, and websites can say what they want, as long as it is true. A newspaper can write true things about the President of the United States, even if the President does not like it.

The Right to Petition the Government

The First Amendment gives us the right to ask for change. We can change laws. We can make complaints to the government if we do not like what the government is doing.

Other Rights

Some of the other nine amendments protect the rights of a person who is arrested. The Fourth Amendment protects people from unreasonable searches. The police need government permission to be able to enter a person's home and search it. The Fifth Amendment protects a person's right to be silent. When a person is arrested, the police cannot make the person speak. The Sixth Amendment promises that all people can have a fast trial, a jury, and the help of a lawyer to represent them.

Read the article. Write *T* for True or *F* for False. Then correct the false sentences.

_____ 1. The twenty-seven amendments of the Constitution are the Bill of Rights.

_____ 2. The First Amendment protects freedom of speech, religion, assembly, press, and the right to petition the government.

_____ 3. Freedom of religion means a person can follow any religion or no religion at all.

_____ 4. Freedom of speech means a person can say his or her ideas out loud but not write them.

_____ 5. Freedom of assembly means people can have parties in their homes.

_____ 6. The freedom to petition the government means people can try to change the laws when they don't like them.

_____ 7. Freedom of the press means newspapers and magazines can print false information.

_____ 8. When someone is arrested, the Bill of Rights takes away a person's rights.

6 READ AND WRITE

A READ. Go to page 174. Read sentences 29–30 aloud and check your pronunciation.

B WRITE. Go to page 176. Listen and write sentences 29–30.

7 CIVICS IN ACTION

DISCUSS. What is protected in the Bill of Rights? How can these protections affect your daily life?

Connect to Your Active Book

Use e-flashcards to prepare for the civics test.

Do the record-and-compare exercises to prepare for the reading test.

Do the writing dictation exercises to prepare for the writing test.

Can you... answer the questions on page 59 about the Bill of Rights? ☐

Lesson 1 The Three Branches of Government

1 GET READY

A T032 🔊 **Listen to the questions. Do you know the answers?**

- Name <u>one</u> branch, or part, of the government. (Question 13)
- Who is in charge of the executive branch? (Question 15)
- Who makes federal laws? (Question 16)
- What are the <u>two</u> parts of the U.S. Congress? (Question 17)

B If you want to check your answers, go to page 202.

2 WHAT DO YOU KNOW?

A Look at the buildings in Washington, D.C. What are their names? Label the pictures. Use the names in the box.

the Capitol	the Supreme Court	the White House

1. _____ 2. _____ 3. _____

B Who works in each building?

A Read the sentences. Do you know the words in bold?

1. The police **enforce** the traffic laws. They can stop you if they see you driving too fast.
2. There are many **regulations** about gift giving. Most leaders cannot receive gifts.
3. A governor **is in charge** of the state government.
4. The courts are in the **judicial** branch.
5. The President is in the **executive** branch.
6. Congress is in the **legislative** branch.
7. The **federal** government is in Washington, D.C. It is the center of the U.S. government.

B Match the words and the definitions.

_____ 1. enforce laws	**a.** government rules
_____ 2. regulations	**b.** have responsibility for something
_____ 3. be in charge of	**c.** make sure that people follow laws
_____ 4. judicial	**d.** related to making laws
_____ 5. executive	**e.** related to making and carrying out decisions
_____ 6. legislative	**f.** of the court
_____ 7. federal	**g.** national

4 **READ**

A 🔊 **T033** Listen and read the article.

B Read the article again. Then complete the chart. Use the words in the box.

the Capitol	Congress	judges
the President	representatives	senators
the Supreme Court	the Vice President	the White House

	Legislative Branch	Executive Branch	Judicial Branch
Place			
People			

The Three Branches of Government

The Founding Fathers wrote the U.S. Constitution, and made sure that no one person or group in the government could have too much power. They separated the government into three parts, or branches: the legislative, the executive, and the judicial. Each branch is equally powerful. No one branch is more powerful than the other.

The Executive Branch

The executive branch enforces laws. That is, it makes sure that people follow the laws. It also writes regulations to make sure businesses and government offices follow the law. The President is in charge of the executive branch. Citizens of the United States elect the President.

Culture Note

State governments also have three branches. The Governor is head of a state's Executive Branch.

The Legislative Branch

The Congress is the legislative branch of the United States. It is also called the U.S. or national legislature. Congress makes federal laws—laws that all the people in the country must follow. There are two parts of Congress: the Senate and the House of Representatives. U.S. citizens from each state vote for senators and representatives to represent them in Congress in Washington, D.C.

The Judicial Branch

The courts are the judicial branch of the U.S. government. The judicial branch explains U.S. laws. The most important court in the judicial branch is the Supreme Court. It is the highest court in the country. The Supreme Court makes sure that the laws in the United States follow the Constitution. The executive and legislative branches decide on who can be a judge in the courts. Citizens do not vote for federal judges.

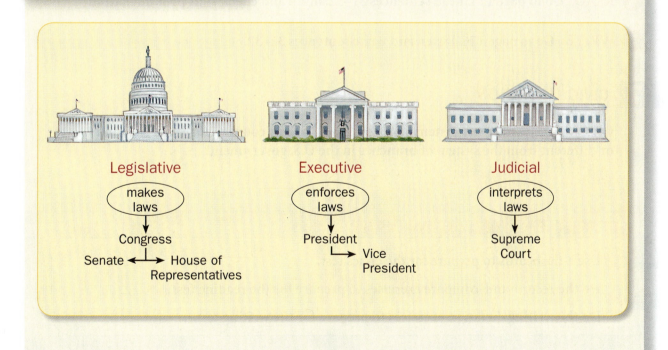

Legislative	Executive	Judicial
makes laws	enforces laws	interprets laws
Congress	President	Supreme Court
Senate ◀▶ House of Representatives	Vice President	

Read the article. Then complete the sentences. Use the words in the box.

Congress	courts	executive	judicial
legislative	President	Senate	three

1. The Constitution separates the powers of the government into _____ parts.

2. The executive branch is made up of the _____, the Vice President, and the Cabinet.

3. The _____ branch makes the laws.

4. The _____ branch enforces the laws.

5. The _____ branch explains the laws.

6. The _____ and the House of Representatives are the two parts of Congress.

7. The _____ are part of the judicial branch of the government.

8. _____ is part of the legislative branch.

A READ. Go to page 174. Read sentences 31–32 aloud and check your pronunciation.

B WRITE. Go to page 176. Listen and write sentences 31–32.

DISCUSS. Describe the system of government in your country. How is it the same or different from the system of branches in the U.S. government?

Connect to Your Active Book

Use e-flashcards to prepare for the civics test.

Do the record-and-compare exercises to prepare for the reading test.

Do the writing dictation exercises to prepare for the writing test.

Can you…answer the questions on page 63 about the system of the U.S. government? ☐

1 GET READY

A T034 🔊 **Listen to the question. Do you know the answer?**

- What stops <u>one</u> branch of government from becoming too powerful? (Question 14)

B If you want to check your answer, go to page 202.

2 WHAT DO YOU KNOW?

Look at the pictures. Who are the people in each picture? What do they do?

Do you know the words in bold? What do they mean? Circle *a* or *b*.

1. The president can **appoint a judge** to the Supreme Court.
   a. recommend a judge   b. fire a judge

2. Most people who break the law go to **prison**. They often stay for years.
   a. school   b. jail

3. The Supreme Court can **annul** a law.
   a. write   b. cancel

4. The president can **pardon** a person for doing a crime.
   a. thank   b. forgive

5. When the president signs a **bill**, it becomes law.
   a. a plan for a law   b. check

6. The Supreme Court is a very **powerful** court. It can change the decisions from other courts.
   a. old   b. strong

4 READ

A T035 🔊 **Listen and read the article.**

B **Read the article again. Then complete the sentences. Use the words in the box.**

checks and balances	courts	legislative branch	President
separation of powers	veto	Supreme Court	

1. The Constitution separates the U.S. government into three branches. This is called _____.

2. Only the President has the power to _____ a law.

3. Only the _____ has the power to write a law.

4. Only the _____ can send a person to prison.

5. Only the _____ can pardon a person in prison.

6. The _____ has the power to cancel a law if it decides it is unconstitutional.

7. The system of _____ stops one branch of government from becoming too powerful.

Keeping a Balance of Power

The Constitution of the United States separates the power of the government into three branches: the executive, the legislative, and the judicial. Each branch has its own powers and responsibilities. This is called the separation of powers. Each branch is limited in what it can do, so no one branch of the government can control the other two branches.

Each branch has ways to check or stop the other branches from becoming too powerful. This is called "checks and balances." Below are three examples of checks and balances.

The separation of powers and the system of checks and balances stops one person or one branch of the government from becoming too powerful. In this way, no one branch of government can take control.

Checks and Balances

Congress writes a law, but the President must sign it to become law. If the President doesn't like the law, he or she can veto it. This means the President can say no and not sign the law. The Supreme Court has the power to annul the law if it decides the law is not constitutional.

The President has the power to appoint a judge to the Supreme Court. Congress has the power to say yes or no to the President's appointment. The Congress also has the power to take the judge off the Supreme Court if the judge does something against the law.

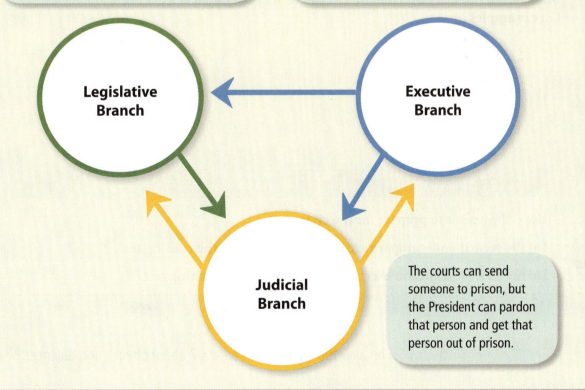

Legislative Branch

Executive Branch

Judicial Branch

The courts can send someone to prison, but the President can pardon that person and get that person out of prison.

5   CHECK YOUR UNDERSTANDING

Read the article. Check (✓) the branches that have power in each situation.

	Executive Branch	Legislative Branch	Judicial Branch
Appointing a judge to the Supreme Court	☐	☐	☐
Making laws	☐	☐	☐
Sending a person to prison	☐	☐	☐

6   READ AND WRITE

A READ. Go to page 175. Read sentences 33–34 aloud and check your pronunciation.

B WRITE. Go to page 177. Listen and write sentences 33–34.

7   CIVICS IN ACTION

DISCUSS. Think about the system of checks and balances provided by the branches in the U.S. government. Do you think the system is working? Give examples.

Connect to Your Active Book

Use e-flashcards to prepare for the civics test.

Do the record-and-compare exercises to prepare for the reading test.

Do the writing dictation exercises to prepare for the writing test.

Can you...answer the question on page 67 about checks and balances? ☐

Lesson 1   The President

1   GET READY

A T036 🔊)) **Listen to the questions. Do you know the answers?**

- We elect a President for how many years? (Question 26)
- In what month do we vote for President? (Question 27)
- What is the name of the President of the United States now? (Question 28)
- Who is the Commander in Chief of the military? (Question 32)
- Who signs bills to become laws? (Question 33)
- Who vetoes bills? (Question 34)

B If you want to check your answers, go to pages 202 and 203.

2   WHAT DO YOU KNOW?

Look at the pictures. What are some responsibilities of the President of the United States?

A Read the sentences. Do you know the words in bold?

1. The President has a **term** of four years.

2. Citizens of the United States **elect** the President.

3. The Congress makes laws. First a congressperson writes a **bill**, then the Congress votes on it.

4. There are five branches in the U.S. **military**: Army, Navy, Air Force, Marines, and Coast Guard.

5. The President can **veto** a bill from Congress if he doesn't like it.

B Match the words and the definitions.

_____ 1. bill   a. to choose someone by voting

_____ 2. elect   b. a period of time

_____ 3. military   c. a plan for a new law

_____ 4. term   d. to say no to a plan

_____ 5. veto   e. organizations that fight for a country

4 READ

A T037 🔊 Listen and read the article.

B Read the article again. Then complete the sentences. Use the words in the box.

Commander in Chief	eight	executive	four
November	signs	vetoes	

1. The first Tuesday of every _____, U.S. citizens vote.

2. Citizens elect the President for _____ years.

3. The President can be in office for a total of _____ years.

4. The President is the _____ of the military.

5. The President is the leader of the _____ branch.

6. The President _____ a bill to make it a law.

7. If the President _____ a bill, it will not become a law.

The President

The first Tuesday of every November is called Election Day. It is the day that U.S. citizens vote. Once every four years on this day, they vote for the President of the United States. The President is the head of the executive branch. The President has the highest office in the U.S. government.

The office of the U.S. President is very powerful. To limit this power, a President can only be in power for two terms. Each term is four years long. After eight years, the President must leave his office.

The President of the United States has many responsibilities. The President is the Commander in Chief of the military. This means that the President has control of the Army, Navy, Air Force, Marines, and Coast Guard. The President makes the final decisions on how to use the military at home and around the world.

The U.S. President is the only one who can sign bills into laws. First Congress writes bills. Members of Congress talk about the bill and make changes to the bill. Then they vote on the bill.

If the bill passes, it goes to the desk of the President. The President can do one of two things: sign the bill into law or veto it. If the President signs the bill, it means that the bill becomes a new law in the United States. If the President vetoes the bill, this means the bill does not become a law. If this happens, the bill has to go back to Congress.

Congress can still try to make the bill a law, but it has to vote on the bill again. This time it has to get two-thirds of Congress to vote yes for the bill. This is hard to do. Only 4 percent of vetoed bills have become laws!

In November 2008, Barack Obama became the 44th President of the United States.

5 CHECK YOUR UNDERSTANDING

Read the article. How does a bill become law? Put the events in order.

_8_ **a.** The bill becomes law.

_____ **b.** Congress votes on the bill.

_____ **c.** The bill passes Congress.

_1_ **d.** Congress writes a bill.

_____ **e.** The President reads the bill.

_____ **f.** Congress talks about the bill and makes changes.

_____ **g.** The President signs the bill.

_____ **h.** The bill goes to the desk of the President.

6 READ AND WRITE

A READ. Go to page 175. Read sentences 35–36 aloud and check your pronunciation.

B WRITE. Go to page 177. Listen and write sentences 35–36.

7 CIVICS IN ACTION

DISCUSS. The U.S. President is in the news every day. What are some of the things the President is working on now? Which issues are of special interest to you?

Connect to Your Active Book

Use e-flashcards to prepare for the civics test.

Do the record-and-compare exercises to prepare for the reading test.

Do the writing dictation exercises to prepare for the writing test.

Can you...answer the questions on page 71 about the President of the United States? ☐

Lesson 2 The Vice President and the Speaker of the House

1 GET READY

A T038 🔊 **Listen to the questions. Do you know the answers?**

- What is the name of the Vice President of the United States now? (Question 29)
- If the President can no longer serve, who becomes President? (Question 30)
- If both the President and the Vice President can no longer serve, who becomes President? (Question 31)
- What is the name of the Speaker of the House of Representatives now? (Question 47)

B If you want to check your answers, go to page 203.

2 WHAT DO YOU KNOW?

Look at the picture. What jobs do these elected officials have?
Can you name some of their responsibilities?

Joseph Biden and Nancy Pelosi are sitting behind Barack Obama. (2010)

A **Read the sentences. Do you know the words in bold?**

1. There are two large **political parties** in the United States: the Republicans and the Democrats.

2. A President can **serve** two terms.

3. There are 435 **members** in the House of Representatives.

4. If the Congress likes the idea for a new law, it **passes the bill**.

5. To be President of the United States, you must be born a U.S. citizen. It is a **requirement**.

B **Match the words and the definitions.**

_____ 1. political party

_____ 2. serve

_____ 3. members

_____ 4. pass a bill

_____ 5. requirement

a. something that you need

b. a group of people with the same political ideas

c. to vote yes on a plan for a law

d. people who belong to a group or organization

e. to spend time doing a job

4   READ

A T039 🔊 **Listen and read the article.**

B **Read the article again. Then complete the sentences. Use the words in the box.**

executive	legislative	second	third	Vice President

1. The Vice President is part of the _____ branch.

2. The Vice President is _____ in line to the president.

3. The Speaker of the House is part of the _____ branch.

4. The Speaker of the House is _____ in line to the President.

5. The _____ votes to break a tie vote in the Senate.

The Second and Third in Command

The Vice President

The head of the executive branch is the President. The Vice President is second in line to the President. If the President can no longer serve, the Vice President becomes President.

The Vice President must meet the same requirements as the President of the United States. The requirements to be President or Vice President are the following: to be at least thirty-five years old; to be a U.S. citizen by birth; and to live in the United States for at least fourteen years.

Vice President Joseph R. Biden, Jr.

The President chooses a person to be his or her Vice President before Election Day. People vote for both the President and Vice President on the same ticket. There is not a separate vote for Vice President.

The Vice President serves as president of the Senate. If the Senate is divided 50-50 on a vote, the Vice President can then vote to break the tie.

The Speaker of the House

The head of the legislative branch is the Speaker of the House. The Speaker of the House is third in line to the President. If both the President and the Vice President can no longer serve, the Speaker of the House becomes President.

The Speaker is a member of the House of Representatives. The political party in control of the House of Representatives chooses the Speaker of the House. The job of the Speaker is to lead the House of Representatives and to help pass bills through Congress.

Nancy Pelosi was the first woman to become Speaker of the House (2007).

Culture Note

Originally, the most important responsibility of the Vice President was to be president of the Senate. Today the Vice President also represents the United States to the world. The Vice President speaks for the President in international meetings.

Read the article. Complete the sentences. Write *Speaker of the House* or *Vice President*.

1. The _____ is the President of the Senate.

2. The _____ is the leader of the House of Representatives.

3. If the President can no longer serve, the _____ becomes President.

4. If the President and the Vice President can no longer serve, the _____ becomes President.

5. Members of the House choose the _____.

6. The _____ votes in the Senate if the Senate is divided 50-50.

7. The _____ and President are on the same ticket on Election Day.

8. To be _____, you must be a citizen by birth and at least thirty-five years old.

6 READ AND WRITE

Ⓐ **READ.** Go to page 175. Read sentences 37–38 aloud and check your pronunciation.

Ⓑ **WRITE.** Go to page 177. Listen and write sentences 37–38.

7 CIVICS IN ACTION

DISCUSS. If the U.S. President can no longer lead the country, the Constitution gives clear instructions on who will become the new President. Why do you think the Constitution includes this information?

Connect to Your Active Book

Use e-flashcards to prepare for the civics test.

Do the record-and-compare exercises to prepare for the reading test.

Do the writing dictation exercises to prepare for the writing test.

Can you... answer the questions on page 75 about the U.S. Vice President and the Speaker of the House?   ☐

LESSON 3 THE U.S. CABINET

1 GET READY

A T040 🔊)) **Listen to the questions. Do you know the answers?**

- What does the President's Cabinet do? (Question 35)
- What are <u>two</u> Cabinet-level positions? (Question 36)

B **If you want to check your answers, go to page 203.**

2 WHAT DO YOU KNOW?

Look at the information. Why does the President need so many people in the Cabinet?

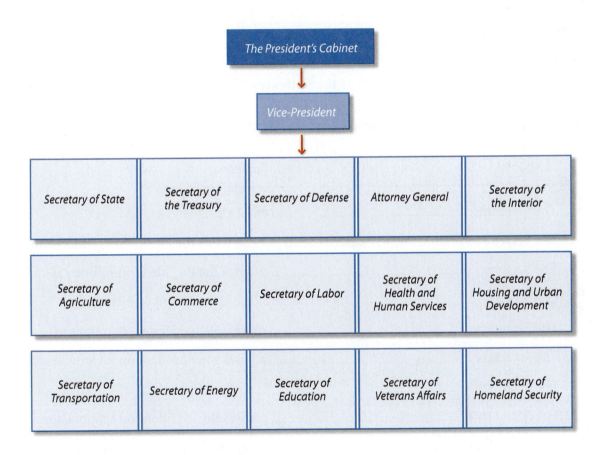

The President's Cabinet				
Vice-President				
Secretary of State	Secretary of the Treasury	Secretary of Defense	Attorney General	Secretary of the Interior
Secretary of Agriculture	Secretary of Commerce	Secretary of Labor	Secretary of Health and Human Services	Secretary of Housing and Urban Development
Secretary of Transportation	Secretary of Energy	Secretary of Education	Secretary of Veterans Affairs	Secretary of Homeland Security

Do you know the words in bold? What do they mean? Circle *a* or *b*.

1. There are fifteen cabinet-level **positions**.
   a. jobs   b. people

2. The President **appoints** a person to be a Cabinet member.
   a. votes for   b. chooses

3. The Senate interviews and **approves** the person.
   a. decides the person is a good choice   b. says good-bye to the person

4. The Cabinet talks to the President about **issues** in the country and world today.
   a. problems   b. activities

5. The Cabinet members **advise** the President.
   a. offer suggestions to the President   b. listen to the President talk

6. A Secretary of the Cabinet **manages** a particular government department.
   a. owns   b. leads

4 **READ**

A T041 🔊)) **Listen and read the article.**

B **Read the article again. Then complete the sentences. Use the words in the box.**

Agriculture	Attorney General	Cabinet
Defense	Education	Homeland Security
Labor	State	Treasury

1. There are fifteen _____ positions.

2. The Secretary of the _____ advises the President on the economy.

3. The Secretary of _____ advises the President on military issues.

4. The _____ is in charge of the Department of Justice.

5. The Secretary of _____ represents the United States to the world.

6. The Secretary of _____ advises the President on farming issues.

7. The Secretary of _____ is a leader in the field of workplace safety.

8. The Secretary of _____ advises the President on school issues.

9. The Secretary of _____ takes care of national security and immigration issues.

The Eyes and Ears of the President

The President is the head of the U.S. government and of the executive branch. The President has many responsibilities and has advisors to help make the right decisions. The U.S. Cabinet is a group of fifteen people who advise the President. The Vice President is also a member of the President's Cabinet. The Cabinet members are leaders in their fields and advise the President on many issues. Their suggestions are very important. They are truly the eyes and ears of the President.

The Role of the Senate

The President chooses the people for the Cabinet, but the Senate must approve them. The Senate interviews each person and decides if that person should become a Cabinet member. Sometimes the Senate does not approve the President's choice. Then the President must appoint a different person, and the process begins again.

The Top Three Cabinet Positions

The Secretary of State advises the President on international issues and represents the United States to the world.

The Secretary of the Treasury advises the President on the economy.

The Secretary of Defense advises the President on the military.

More Cabinet Positions

The Attorney General is the head of the Department of Justice and is in charge of law enforcement, prisons, and the FBI.

The Secretary of the Interior manages all national land and parks.

The Secretary of Agriculture advises the President on farming and food safety issues.

The Secretary of Commerce advises the President on business issues.

The Secretary of Labor advises the President on workplace laws and safety.

The Secretary of Health and Human Services is responsible for all basic health services including Medicare and Medicaid, the Centers for Disease Control, and the Food and Drug Administration.

The Secretary of Housing and Urban Development is responsible for loan programs and public housing.

The Secretary of Transportation manages all national transportation including airports.

The Secretary of Energy is responsible for energy research and also the safety of nuclear energy.

The Secretary of Education advises the President on issues in education for both children and adults.

The Secretary of Veterans Affairs makes sure people who fought in American wars get their benefits.

The Secretary of Homeland Security advises the President on problems in national security and immigration. This position was created after 9/11.

President Obama, Vice President Biden, the Cabinet, and White House staff (2009)

Culture Note

There were only three members in President Washington's first Cabinet: the Secretary of War, the Secretary of the Treasury, and the Attorney General.

5 CHECK YOUR UNDERSTANDING

Read the article. Write *T* for True or *F* for False. Then correct the false sentences.

_____ 1. The Cabinet always has fifteen members.

_____ 2. The Cabinet members are leaders in their fields.

_____ 3. U.S. citizens vote for the Cabinet members.

_____ 4. The Senate can say no to a person the President appoints to the Cabinet.

_____ 5. The top three Cabinet positions are Secretary of State, Secretary of Defense, and Secretary of the Treasury.

_____ 6. The Cabinet members are part of the legislative branch of the government.

_____ 7. The Secretary of State advises the President on the economy.

_____ 8. The Secretary of Defense advises the President on the military.

6 READAND WRITE

A READ. Go to page 175. Read sentences 39–40 aloud and check your pronunciation.

B WRITE. Go to page 177. Listen and write sentences 39–40.

7 CIVICS IN ACTION

DISCUSS. Review the descriptions of the Cabinet offices on page 81. Make a list of different ways their responsibilities and services affect you and your community.

Connect to Your Active Book

Use e-flashcards to prepare for the civics test.

Do the record-and-compare exercises to prepare for the reading test.

Do the writing dictation exercises to prepare for the writing test.

Can you... answer the questions on page 79 about the U.S. Cabinet? ☐

Lesson 1 The Senate

1 GET READY

A **T042** 🔊 **Listen to the questions. Do you know the answers?**

- How many U.S. Senators are there? (Question 18)
- We elect a U.S. Senator for how many years? (Question 19)
- Who is <u>one</u> of your state's U.S. Senators now? (Question 20)
- Who does a U.S. Senator represent? (Question 24)

B **If you want to check your answers, go to page 202.**

2 WHAT DO YOU KNOW?

Look at the picture. What is the name of this building? Where is it?

A Read the sentences. Do you know the words in bold?

1. Puerto Rico and Guam are two **territories** of the United States.
2. The power of the Senate **balances** the power of the President.
3. The **committee** studies the law carefully then explains it to the Congress.
4. Senators **represent** their states in Congress.
5. Congress writes **bills**, which then become laws.

B Match the words and the definitions.

_____ 1. territory   **a.** to speak for other people

_____ 2. balance   **b.** land that is controlled by a distant country

_____ 3. committee   **c.** make things equal

_____ 4. represent   **d.** a group of people chosen to do a particular job

_____ 5. bill   **e.** a plan for a new law

4 READ

A 🔊 T043 Listen and read the article.

B Read the article again. Then complete the sentences. Use the words in the box.

bill	Congress	pass	Senate	senators	territories

1. _____ is the legislative branch of the U.S. government.

2. The U.S. _____ has 100 members.

3. Each state sends two _____ to Congress.

4. U.S. _____ do not send senators to Congress.

5. A member of Congress can write a _____, which may become a law.

6. If members of Congress _____ a bill, it goes to the President to become a law.

The Senate

There are three branches of government in the United States: judicial, executive, and legislative. The legislative branch makes the laws. Congress is the legislative branch. Congress has two chambers: the House of Representatives and the Senate.

The Senate is the smaller part of Congress, but it is very powerful. There are 100 U.S. senators. Voters in each state send two senators to the Senate. It doesn't matter how many people live in the state, each state has only two senators. Senators represent all the people from a state. People who live in U.S. territories, such as Puerto Rico or Guam, do not have senators.

The Senate makes laws. It also interviews the people the President appoints to the Supreme Court and the President's Cabinet. The power the Senate has over the Cabinet and Supreme Court balances the power of the President. It is part of the checks and balances system in the U.S. Constitution.

A senator must be at least thirty years old, a U.S. citizen for at least nine years, and living in the state to be represented. Senators are elected for six years. There are no term limits.

Senator Edward Kennedy, a Democrat from Massachusetts, served for forty-six years.

Octaviano Larrazolo, Republican, was the first Hispanic elected to the Senate.

Culture Note

The Senate divides its work among many committees, or small groups of Senators. Each committee has a special interest in and understanding of a topic; for example, the military, healthcare, banking, etc. Each committee studies and writes laws in its special area.

How a Law is Made in the Senate

1. A senator has an idea for a new law (a bill).

2. A senator introduces the bill.

3. The Senate sends the bill to a committee. The small group discusses the bill.

4. The committee approves the bill.

5. The Senate talks about the bill, makes some changes, and votes on it.

6. If the bill passes, it goes to the House of Representatives.*

7. The House talks about the bill, makes some changes, and votes on it.

8. The bill returns to the Senate, where members talk about it, make some changes, and vote on it again.

9. After both chambers of Congress have passed the final bill, it goes to the President.

10. The President can sign the bill into law or veto the bill.

*A law can start in the Senate or the House.

A   Read the article. Write the answers to the questions.

1. How many senators represent each state? _____

2. How many senators are in the Senate? _____

3. How long is a senator's term? _____

4. How many terms can a senator serve? _____

5. Who votes for a senator? _____

B   Read the article again. Put the events in order.

How a law is made in the Senate

_____ **a.** The bill goes to the President to become a law.

__1__ **b.** A person has an idea for a law.

_____ **c.** The bill is introduced to the Senate.

_____ **d.** The bill passes the Senate and the House.

_____ **e.** The Senate talks about the bill and makes changes to it.

_____ **f.** The bill goes to the House. It passes.

6   READ AND WRITE

A   READ.   Go to page 175. Read sentences 41–42 aloud and check your pronunciation.

B   WRITE.   Go to page 177. Listen and write sentences 41–42.

7   CIVICS IN ACTION

DISCUSS.   Think of an issue affecting your community. What kind of bill could your senator take to Congress that would be helpful?

Connect to Your Active Book

Use e-flashcards to prepare for the civics test.

Do the record-and-compare exercises to prepare for the reading test.

Do the writing dictation exercises to prepare for the writing test.

Can you...answer the questions on page 83 about the Senate?   ☐

LESSON 2 THE HOUSE OF REPRESENTATIVES

1 GET READY

A T044 🔊)) Listen to the questions. Do you know the answers?

- The House of Representatives has how many voting members? (Question 21)
- We elect a U.S. Representative for how many years? (Question 22)
- Name your U.S. Representative. (Question 23)
- Why do some states have more Representatives than other states? (Question 25)

B If you want to check your answers, go to page 202.

2 WHAT DO YOU KNOW?

Look at the picture. Who are the people? Where are they?

Do you know the words in bold? Complete the sentences. Circle _a_ or _b_.

1. California has a **population** _____.
   a. of 3 million square miles
   b. of 36 million people

2. Every ten years, the United States conducts a **census** _____.
   a. to find out how many people live here
   b. to elect a new president

3. Every member of the House represents a **district**, which can be a large or small _____.
   a. area
   b. country

4. **Delegates** are people who _____ the U.S. territories.
   a. visit
   b. represent

5. A voting member of the **House of Representatives** can _____.
   a. talk about a bill
   b. vote on a bill

4 READ

T045
A 🔊 **Listen and read the article.**

B **Read the article again. Then complete the sentences. Use the words in the box.**

census	delegates	district
House of Representatives	legislative branch	population
representatives		

1. Congress is the _____ of the U.S. government.

2. There are two parts of Congress: the Senate and the _____ .

3. There are 435 _____ in the House of Representatives.

4. Each member of the House of Representatives serves a _____ in the United States.

5. Every ten years a government _____ counts all the people who live in the United States.

6. Some states have more representatives because they have a bigger

   _____ .

7. _____ from the U.S. territories do not vote in Congress, but they represent the people in the territories.

The House of Representatives

There are three branches of government in the United States: judicial, executive, and legislative. The legislative branch makes the laws. Congress is the legislative branch. Congress has two chambers: the House of Representatives and the Senate.

The House of Representatives

The House is the larger part of Congress. There are 435 members in the House of Representatives. The number of representatives from each state is based on the state's population. When the U.S. Constitution was written, there was one representative for every 30,000 people. Today each representative represents between 600,000 and 700,000 people.

In states with small populations, there is only one representative. There are six states with just one representative: Alaska, Delaware, North Dakota, South Dakota, Vermont, and Wyoming. Other states have more representatives because they have more people. For example, California has fifty-three representatives.

When there is more than one representative for a state, each representative works for a specific district inside the state. He or she is not responsible for the whole state.

The number of representatives for each state changes if the population in a state changes. Every ten years, the U.S. government does a census. It tries to count every person in the country. The information from the census decides how many representatives each state can have.

In 1870, Joseph Rainey–a former slave–was the first African-American elected to the House of Representatives.

Representative Requirements

A Representative must be at least twenty-five years old, a U.S. citizen for at least seven years, and live in the district. Representatives are elected for two years. They can be reelected many times. Some representatives have served in Congress for over fifty years!

The Territories

People who live in U.S. territories (Puerto Rico or Guam) or the District of Columbia (Washington, D.C.) have delegates in the House of Representatives, but they cannot vote. In other words, the territories have no voting representatives in Congress. Delegates from territories can start bills and discuss bills, but they cannot vote on the bills.

> ### Culture Note
> In 1917, Jeanette Rankin —often called the "Lady of the House"— became the first female representative.

Read the article. Then answer the questions. Circle *a, b,* or *c.*

1. How many members are there in the House of Representatives?
   a. 50   **b.** 100   **c.** 435

2. How long is one term for a representative?
   a. two years   **b.** four years   **c.** six years

3. Where does the House of Representatives meet?
   a. in the White House   **b.** in Washington, D.C.   **c.** in representatives' districts

4. What does the House of Representatives do?
   a. It counts U.S. citizens.   **b.** It makes laws.   **c.** It approves Cabinet members.

5. Which branch is the House of Representatives part of?
   a. the judicial branch   **b.** the executive branch   **c.** the legislative branch

6. Who votes for a representative?
   a. any citizen in the representative's district   **b.** any citizen in the state   **c.** any citizen in the U.S.

---

6 READ AND WRITE

A READ. **Go to page 175. Read sentences 43–44 aloud and check your pronunciation.**

B WRITE. **Go to page 177. Listen and write sentences 43–44.**

---

7 CIVICS IN ACTION

DISCUSS. **Who is your congressional representative? Do you know where his or her office is in your district? Which days and times can you meet with him or her? What are other ways to contact your representative?**

Connect to Your Active Book

Use e-flashcards to prepare for the civics test.

Do the record-and-compare exercises to prepare for the reading test.

Do the writing dictation exercises to prepare for the writing test.

Can you...answer the questions on page 87 about the House of Representatives? ☐

1 GET READY

A T046 🔊 **Listen to the questions. Do you know the answers?**

- What does the judicial branch do? (Question 37)
- What is the highest court in the United States? (Question 38)
- How many justices are on the Supreme Court? (Question 39)
- Who is the Chief Justice of the United States now? (Question 40)

B **If you want to check your answers, go to page 203.**

2 WHAT DO YOU KNOW?

Look at the picture. What is the name of this building? Where is it?

A   Read the paragraph. Do you know the words in bold?

> Courts in the United States listen to **disputes** between people, and they **resolve** disagreements. Courts review **cases** and make decisions. This means a court **rules** on a case. If the people in the case do not like the decision, they can **appeal** it. There are nine **justices** on the Supreme Court. The leader is the **Chief Justice**. The President decides who will be Chief Justice.

B   Match the words and the definitions.

_____ **1.** a dispute	**a.** the leader of a group
_____ **2.** resolve	**b.** something a court of law must decide
_____ **3.** case	**c.** disagreement
_____ **4.** rule	**d.** to ask a more important court to change another court's decision
_____ **5.** appeal	**e.** to make a court decision
_____ **6.** justice	**f.** a judge in the Supreme Court
_____ **7.** chief	**g.** to end a disagreement

4   READ

A   T047 🔊 Listen and read the article.

B   Read the article again. Then complete the sentences. Use the words in the box.

Constitution	judicial branch	justices
President	review	Supreme Court

1. The courts are part of the _____ of the U.S. government.

2. The courts _____ and explain laws.

3. The _____ is the highest court in the United States.

4. There are nine _____ on the Supreme Court.

5. The Supreme Court decides if a law is against the _____.

6. The _____ chooses the Chief Justice.

The Federal Court System

The U.S. government has three branches: executive, legislative, and judicial. The President, the Vice President, and the Cabinet are part of the executive branch. The executive branch makes sure laws are followed. The Congress is the legislative branch. It makes laws. The courts are the judicial branch. The judicial branch reviews and explains laws.

Three Levels of Courts

The judicial branch resolves disputes or disagreements. There are three levels of federal courts in the United States. A case begins in the district courts. If a person does not like a court's decision, he or she can appeal the case in the Court of Appeals. If the person does not like the decision from the Court of Appeals, he or she can ask the Supreme Court to review the case. The Supreme Court is the highest court in the United States. Its decision is final.

Every year, many cases are sent to the Supreme Court. The Supreme Court listens to and rules on about ninety cases a year. The Supreme Court decides if a case or law goes against the Constitution. The justices hear both sides of the dispute, then they vote on the case. Each justice has one vote. The side with five or more votes wins the case.

The Nine Justices

There are nine justices on the Supreme Court. One is the Chief Justice, who is the head of the judicial branch of the United States. He or she has some extra responsibilities but does not have a stronger vote than the other eight justices.

Becoming a Justice on the Supreme Court

Citizens do not elect the justices; the President appoints the justices to the Supreme Court. Then the Senate meets to approve them. Sometimes the Senate does not approve the president's choice. Then the President must appoint a different person.

The decision to appoint a justice is a very big decision. The Supreme Court justices can serve for life. Once appointed to the Supreme Court, the justice serves until retirement or death. Most justices serve for about twenty-five years.

The Federal Court System

U.S. Supreme Court
↑
U.S. Courts of Appeals
↑
U.S. District Courts

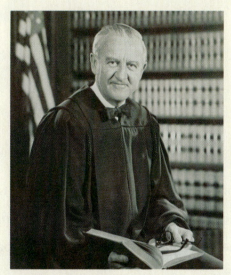

Justice John Paul Stevens served until he was ninety years old.

Read the article. Write *T* for True or *F* for False. Then correct the false sentences.

_____ **1.** The Supreme Court is the highest court.

_____ **2.** A person can appeal a Supreme Court decision.

_____ **3.** People elect the Supreme Court justices.

_____ **4.** The Senate can say no to a justice the President appoints.

_____ **5.** The President can take a justice off the Supreme Court.

_____ **6.** The justices can stay on the Supreme Court for as long as they want.

_____ **7.** Each Supreme Court justice has one vote.

_____ **8.** The justices always agree with each other.

6 READ AND WRITE

A READ. **Go to page 175. Read sentences 45–46 aloud and check your pronunciation.**

B WRITE. **Go to page 177. Listen and write sentences 45–46.**

7 CIVICS IN ACTION

DISCUSS. **What are some recent decisions made by the Supreme Court? Do any of these decisions affect you or your community? How?**

Connect to Your Active Book

Use e-flashcards to prepare for the civics test.

Do the record-and-compare exercises to prepare for the reading test.

Do the writing dictation exercises to prepare for the writing test.

Can you… answer the questions on page 91 about the Supreme Court? ☐

LESSON 1   FEDERAL VS. STATE GOVERNMENT

1 GET READY

T048

A **Listen to the questions. Do you know the answers?**

- Under our Constitution, some powers belong to the federal government. What is <u>one</u> power of the federal government? (Question 41)

- Under our Constitution, some powers belong to the states. What is <u>one</u> power of the states? (Question 42)

- What is the capital of the United States? (Question 94)

B If you want to check your answers, go to pages 203 and 206.

2 WHAT DO YOU KNOW?

Look at the pictures. Which services are the responsibilities of the federal government? Of a state government?

Printing money

Police protection

Education

The armed forces

Do you know the words in bold? What do they mean? Circle *a* or *b*.

1. The **capital** of the United States is Washington, D.C.
   - a. center of the government
   - b. national park

2. The government **provides** services such as police protection and fire safety.
   - a. asks for
   - b. gives

3. Congress has the power to **declare war** on another country.
   - a. officially end a war
   - b. officially start a war

4. Countries make **treaties** with other countries to end wars.
   - a. agreements
   - b. business

5. Congress **creates** new laws every year.
   - a. stops
   - b. makes

6. The voters liked the plan. They **approved** it.
   - a. voted for
   - b. vetoed

4 READ

A T049 🔊)) **Listen and read the article.**

B Read the article again. Then identify the responsibilities of the federal and state governments. Write *Federal* or *State*.

_____ **1.** create an army

_____ **2.** issue a driver's license

_____ **3.** provide fire departments

_____ **4.** print money

_____ **5.** provide police

_____ **6.** provide schooling and education

_____ **7.** make treaties and declare war

_____ **8.** approve zoning and land use

Federal Rights and States' Rights

The Founding Fathers did not want a strong central government. For many years they fought against a king who tried to control their state governments. In 1787, when the Founding Fathers wrote the Constitution of the United States, they separated the government's powers. They created a limited federal government. They believed the states should have power, too.

Federal Rights

The Constitution gives some important powers to the federal government. It gives the federal government the power to print money and to operate the postal service. The federal government also has the power to declare war, create an army, and make treaties—agreements—with other countries.

The federal government makes its decisions in the capital of the United States. The capital of the United States is Washington, D.C.

President Gorbachev (USSR) and President Reagan (U.S.), 1987

States' Rights

The states have many powers. States provide protection, such as the police. The states also provide safety, such as fire departments. States make decisions about educating children; they provide schooling and education. States decide on the legal age for marriage and provide marriage licenses. States issue driver's licenses and they have their own traffic laws.

States also make decisions about land use. They approve zoning laws, which decide where buildings can go and how land is used. This means each state controls its growth. These important decisions are made in state capitals across the United States.

Federal and States' Rights

There are also some powers that both the federal government and the states have. They both can increase and collect taxes. They both can pass laws. However, any laws or taxes cannot go against the U.S. Constitution. The U.S. Constitution is always the supreme law of the land.

Culture Note

The first U.S. capital was New York City. Then it was Philadelphia. In 1800, Washington, D.C., became the final home of the United States government.

Read the article. Complete the sentences. Circle *a* or *b*.

1. Originally, the Founding Fathers did not want a strong _____ government.
   a. capital
   b. federal

2. The Founding Fathers separated power between the state and federal _____.
   a. taxes
   b. governments

3. State laws must follow the _____.
   a. Constitution
   b. army

4. The federal government has the power to start and end _____.
   a. a marriage
   b. a war

5. Both state governments and the federal government can _____.
   a. raise taxes
   b. give driver's licenses

6. A state government controls its police, fire departments, and _____.
   a. schools
   b. treaties

A READ. Go to page 175. Read sentences 47–48 aloud and check your pronunciation.

B WRITE. Go to page 177. Listen and write sentences 47–48.

DISCUSS. The Founding Fathers separated the powers of the state and federal governments. Do you think this was a good idea? Why or why not?

Connect to Your Active Book

Use e-flashcards to prepare for the civics test.

Do the record-and-compare exercises to prepare for the reading test.

Do the writing dictation exercises to prepare for the writing test.

Can you... answer the questions on page 95 about the federal and state governments? ☐

1 GET READY

A T050 🔊 Listen to the questions. Do you know the answers?

- Who is the governor of your state now? (Question 43)
- What is the capital of your state? (Question 44)

B If you want to check your answers, go to page 203.

2 WHAT DO YOU KNOW?

A Study the map of the United States on page 190. Point to your state and capital.

B Look at the state quarters. Each quarter gives information about the state. Do you know what information is on quarters from other states?

Washington

Ohio

Texas

Florida

3 BEFORE YOU READ

A Read the sentences. Do you know the words in bold?

1. Most governors can serve two **terms** of four years.

2. National and state governments are **similar**. They both have three branches of government: legislative, executive, and judicial.

3. Many states **limit** the number of years a person can be governor.

4. Alaska has about 700,000 **residents**. Florida has about 18 million people.

5. Every state must follow its **budget**. It is against federal law for states to spend more money than they have.

B Match the words and the definitions.

_____ 1. budget   **a.** a designated period of time

_____ 2. limit   **b.** someone who lives in a particular place

_____ 3. resident   **c.** a plan for how much money can be spent

_____ 4. similar   **d.** to stop something from getting bigger

_____ 5. term   **e.** almost the same but not exactly

4 READ

A T051 🔊 Listen and read the article.

B Read the article again. Then complete the sentences. Use the words in the box.

capital	elect	federal	governor	legislative	taxes

1. The _____ is the head of the state's executive branch.

2. State senators and state representatives work in the _____ branch of the state government.

3. States must follow _____ laws.

4. A state _____ is the home of a state government.

5. States control their own _____ and budgets.

6. People who live in a state _____ their governor.

Fifty States in the Union

There are fifty states in the United States. Washington, D.C., is the capital of the country and home of the federal government.

State governments are very similar to the federal government. Each state has its own constitution. Each state has three branches of government: executive, legislative, and judicial. The capital of your state is the home for your state's government. Each state has its own laws and its own capital.

The Governor

The governor is the head of the executive branch in your state. Governors are usually elected for a term of four years. A governor is elected by the people living in the state. Residents from other states cannot vote in your state elections. Most states limit a governor to two terms.

State Laws

Most states have a state House of Representatives and a state Senate. State representatives and state senators meet in their state capital to write bills and pass laws. The number of terms for state senators and state representatives is different in each state.

States have control over their laws and budgets. States make decisions about their schools and education. Some states say all children must go to school until age eighteen. Other states let children stop school at the age of sixteen. All states make decisions about taxes. They can have different types of taxes. For example, some states do not have an income tax. Other states do not have a tax on food. Some states do not have a tax on clothing.

Iowa Capitol Building

The Texas State Capitol Building in Austin, Texas

New Mexico State Capitol

5 CHECK YOUR UNDERSTANDING

Read the article. Write *T* for True or *F* for False. Then correct the false sentences.

_____ **1.** All states have the same laws.

_____ **2.** Each state has a constitution.

_____ **3.** Only state residents can vote for governor of their state.

_____ **4.** The governor is the head of the federal government.

_____ **5.** State senators work in Washington, D.C.

_____ **6.** Each state has three branches of government.

_____ **7.** States usually have term limits on governors.

_____ **8.** All U.S. residents pay the same taxes.

_____ **9.** The state capital is the home of the federal government.

6 READ AND WRITE

A **READ.** Go to page 175. Read sentences 49–50 aloud and check your pronunciation.

B **WRITE.** Go to page 177. Listen and write sentences 49–50.

7 CIVICS IN ACTION

DISCUSS. The governor of your state is often in the news. Make a list of issues the governor is working on now. Which issues affect you or your community the most?

Connect to Your Active Book

Use e-flashcards to prepare for the civics test.

Do the record-and-compare exercises to prepare for the reading test.

Do the writing dictation exercises to prepare for the writing test.

Can you... answer the questions on page 99 about your state? ☐

1 GET READY

A T052 🔊 Listen to the questions. Do you know the answers?

- What are the <u>two</u> major political parties in the United States? (Question 45)
- What is the political party of the President now? (Question 46)

B If you want to check your answers, go to page 203.

2 WHAT DO YOU KNOW?

Look at the picture of a voting machine. Who did the voter choose?

A Read the paragraph. Do you know the words in bold?

> John McCain was a **candidate** for President in 2008. He **ran for office** against Barack Obama. Mr. McCain and Mr. Obama were the two **major** candidates for President. There were also some other candidates from smaller political **parties**. Most voters in the United States, however, join one of the two major parties: the Democrats or the Republicans. In 2008, Obama, a Democrat, won the election.

B Match the words and the definitions.

_____ 1. candidate   **a.** very large or important

_____ 2. join   **b.** a group of people with the same political ideas

_____ 3. major   **c.** to become a member of a group

_____ 4. party   **d.** to try to get elected

_____ 5. run for office   **e.** someone who wants to be elected

4 READ

A T053 ◀)) Listen and read the article.

B Read the article again. Then complete the sentences. Use the words in the box.

citizens	Democratic	Election Day
party members	Primary Election	Republican

1. Barack Obama is a member of the _____ party.

2. John McCain is a member of the _____ party.

3. Many candidates run against each other in the _____ .

4. _____ is the first Tuesday in November.

5. Only _____ vote in Primary Elections.

6. All U.S. _____ can vote in a national election.

Political Parties in the United States

There were no political parties when the Constitution was written. Our early presidents did not belong to a political party. How did elections work? The person who received the most votes was President, and the person with the second highest number of votes was Vice President.

Over time, people created political parties. Today, there are two major political parties in the United States. They are the Democratic Party and the Republican Party. There are also other smaller parties called third parties. The most recent third parties are the Green Party and the Libertarian Party. U.S. citizens are not required to belong to a political party. A person can be an independent. About 30 percent of Americans call themselves independents. History tells us, however, that most politicians belong to one of the two major parties.

Usually more than one person in a party wants to run for office. The party has a primary election to decide who will be the party's candidate. In a primary election, only party members can vote. Only registered Democrats can vote in a Democratic primary election, and only registered Republicans can vote in a Republican primary election.

In the 1860s, Thomas Nast created the political symbols we know today. The elephant represents the Republican party. The donkey represents the Democratic party.

In 2008, ten different people wanted to be the Democratic presidential candidate. From January to June 2008, every state had a Democratic primary election. Barack Obama won most of the states, so he became the presidential candidate for the Democratic Party. The Republican Party went through the same steps. John McCain became its candidate for President. On the first Tuesday in November 2008, Barack Obama received the most votes and became the forty-fourth President of the United States.

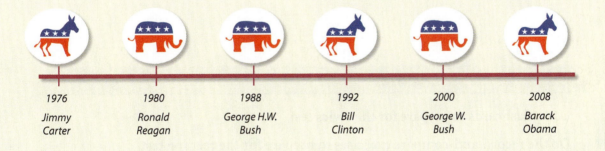

1976	1980	1988	1992	2000	2008
Jimmy Carter	*Ronald Reagan*	*George H.W. Bush*	*Bill Clinton*	*George W. Bush*	*Barack Obama*

5 CHECK YOUR UNDERSTANDING

Read the article. Then answer the questions. Circle *a*, *b*, or *c*.

1. What are the two major political parties in the United States?
   - **a.** McCain and Obama
   - **b.** donkeys and elephants
   - **c.** Democrats and Republicans

2. Which group is an example of a third party?
   - **a.** Libertarians
   - **b.** Republicans
   - **c.** Democrats

3. Why do the major parties have primary elections?
   - **a.** to choose candidates
   - **b.** to elect a president
   - **c.** to join a political party

4. What do we call a person who does not join a political party?
   - **a.** an independent
   - **b.** a citizen
   - **c.** a voter

5. Of the last six U.S. presidents, how many were Democrats?
   - **a.** one
   - **b.** three
   - **c.** two

6. Of the last six U.S. presidents, how many were Republicans?
   - **a.** one
   - **b.** two
   - **c.** three

6 READ AND WRITE

A READ. Go to page 175. Read sentences 51–52 aloud and check your pronunication.

B WRITE. Go to page 177. Listen and write sentences 51–52.

7 CIVICS IN ACTION

DISCUSS. **What do you know about the political parties in the United States? How are they the same? How are they different?**

Connect to Your Active Book

Use e-flashcards to prepare for the civics test.

Do the record-and-compare exercises to prepare for the reading test.

Do the writing dictation exercises to prepare for the writing test.

Can you... answer the questions on page 103 about political parties in the United States? ☐

LESSON 1   BASIC RIGHTS

1   GET READY

A T054 🔊 **Listen to the questions. Do you know the answers?**

- There are four amendments to the Constitution about who can vote. Describe <u>one</u> of them. (Question 48)
- Name <u>one</u> right only for United States citizens. (Question 50)
- What are <u>two</u> rights of everyone living in the United States? (Question 51)
- How old do citizens have to be to vote for President? (Question 54)

B If you want to check your answers, go to pages 203 and 204.

2   WHAT DO YOU KNOW?

Look at the pictures. What are the people doing?

3 BEFORE YOU READ

A Do you know the words in bold? Read the definitions.

1. **run for office** to try to get elected
2. **amendment** a change to the words in the Constitution
3. **apply** to formally ask for something in writing
4. **worship** to pray to a god or religious leader
5. **federal** part of the central government
6. **supreme** highest, best, most important

B Complete the sentences. Use the words in the box.

amendments	apply	federal	run for office	supreme	worship

1. Every four years, people who want to be President _____.

2. Over the years, Congress has made small changes to the Constitution. There are twenty-seven _____ to the Constitution.

3. The Constitution is the _____ law in the United States.

4. There are many religions in the world and many different ways to _____.

5. Anyone can _____ for a job, but only one person gets the job.

6. People who work for the _____ government live in or around Washington, D.C.

4 READ

A T055 🔊) Listen and read the article.

B Read the article again. Match the freedoms and the examples.

_____ 1. freedom of expression and speech   **a.** You can have a meeting in public.

_____ 2. freedom of assembly   **b.** You can have a gun.

_____ 3. freedom to petition the government   **c.** You can follow any religion you want.

_____ 4. freedom of worship   **d.** You can say what you believe.

_____ 5. the right to bear arms   **e.** You can try to change a law.

Constitutional Rights

The U.S. Constitution is the supreme law of the land. It defines the U.S. government. It also defines the basic rights of people living in the United States.

Rights of Everyone Living in the United States

Some people living in the United States are not citizens, but their basic freedoms are protected by the U.S. Constitution.

- Everyone living in the United States has freedom of expression and freedom of speech. This means we can say what we believe. We can disagree with the government.

- Everyone also has the freedom to petition the government. We can ask for change. We can make complaints to the government if we do not like what the government is doing.

- Everyone has the freedom of assembly. This means we are free to have meetings in public, for example: in parks, schools, and government centers.

- Everyone living in the United States has the freedom of religion. This means we can follow any religion or not follow a religion at all. We are free to choose.

- Everyone has the right to bear arms, which means that we can have guns as long as we follow the gun laws in our state.

Rights of U.S. Citizens

There are some rights that are special to U.S. citizens. The most important one is the right to vote. Today any citizen eighteen years old or older can vote. This was not always true. There are four amendments to the Constitution saying who can vote.

Amendments to the Right to Vote

In 1787, only people who owned land could vote. After the slaves were freed, Congress amended the Constitution and said a male citizen of any race can vote. In 1920 Congress added an amendment that said any citizen can vote, in other words, women and men can vote.

For many years, some states stopped poor black people from voting. These states made people pay taxes to vote. Only people with money could vote. In 1964, Congress wrote an amendment that said you don't have to pay a poll tax to vote. All citizens can vote.

In the 1900s some states required voters to be twenty-one years old. Many people thought this was not fair because young men were sent to war at age eighteen. In 1971, Congress passed an amendment that said any citizen eighteen or older can vote.

Other Rights of U.S. Citizens

In addition to the right to vote, U.S. citizens also have the right to run for political office. Naturalized citizens can become Governors, Representatives, or Senators, but a citizen has to be born in the United States to become President or Vice President.

Read the article. Which rights do only citizens have? Which rights are for everyone living in the United States? Write *Citizens* or *Everyone*.

_____ **1.** freedom of assembly

_____ **2.** right to vote

_____ **3.** freedom of speech

_____ **4.** right to run for political office

_____ **5.** freedom of worship

_____ **6.** right to bear arms

_____ **7.** freedom to petition the government

_____ **8.** right to carry a U.S. passport

_____ **9.** right to apply for a federal job

_____ **10.** freedom of expression

6 READ AND WRITE

A READ. Go to page 175. Read sentences 53–54 aloud and check your pronunciation.

B WRITE. Go to page 177. Listen and write sentences 53–54.

7 CIVICS IN ACTION

DISCUSS. In the article, review the rights for everyone living in the United States. Which right is most important to you? Why?

Connect to Your Active Book

Use e-flashcards to prepare for the civics test.

Do the record-and-compare exercises to prepare for the reading test.

Do the writing dictation exercises to prepare for the writing test.

Can you... answer the questions on page 107 about rights in the United States? ☐

LESSON 2 MORE RIGHTS AND RESPONSIBILITIES

1 GET READY

T056

A 🔊 **Listen to the questions. Do you know the answers?**

- What is <u>one</u> responsibility that is only for United States citizens? (Question 49)
- What is <u>one</u> promise you make when you become a United States citizen? (Question 53)
- What are <u>two</u> ways that Americans can participate in their democracy? (Question 55)
- When is the last day you can send in federal income tax forms? (Question 56)
- When must all men register for the Selective Service? (Question 57)

B **If you want to check your answers, go to pages 203 and 204.**

2 WHAT DO YOU KNOW?

Look at the pictures. What is happening in each picture?

Join a civic group in your community.

You can give an elected official your opinion.

Help with a political campaign.

A Read the sentences. Do you know the words in bold?

1. The presidential **campaign** is the biggest and longest political event in the U.S.
2. Always **obey** the law. Don't get in trouble.
3. Citizens can **oppose** a new law. They can say if they don't like it.
4. Citizens must **register** before they can vote. There are many ways to sign up.
5. The military **defends** our country.
6. The military is **loyal** to the president. It always follows the president's decisions.

B Match the words and the definitions.

_____ 1. campaign

_____ 2. obey

_____ 3. oppose

_____ 4. register

_____ 5. defend

_____ 6. loyal

a. to do what a rule or law tells you to do

b. always supportive and following a person or idea

c. meetings and events to help a candidate win an election

d. to disagree with an idea or action

e. to protect something from attack

f. to put your name on an official list

4 READ

A T057 ◀))) Listen and read the article.

B Read the article again. Then complete the sentences. Use the words in the box.

civic groups	defend	elected officials	federal	jury	Selective Service

1. Many citizens serve on a _____ in a court at least one time in their life.

2. In every community, there are many_____ such as neighborhood organizations and clubs.

3. The presidential election is a _____ election.

4. Representatives and senators are _____.

5. The _____ is a list of names of men living in the United States between the ages of eighteen and twenty-six.

6. New citizens promise to _____ the Constitution.

Our Civic Responsibilities

The Promises New Citizens Make

New U.S. citizens promise to be loyal to the United States. This means they support only the U.S. government and give up loyalty to other countries.

New citizens promise to defend the Constitution and laws of the United States. This means they promise to obey the laws of the United States. They also promise to serve or do important work for the nation—even serve in the U.S. military, if needed.

The Responsibilities of U.S. Citizens

Every four years, we have presidential elections. Only U.S. citizens can vote. Citizens should vote in a federal election.

Sometimes U.S. citizens must serve on a jury. As a jury member they help make a decision in a court trial. It is an important responsibility.

A lawyer and a jury in a courtroom

The Responsibilities of Citizens and Non-Citizens

At the age of eighteen all men must register for Selective Service. If there is a war, the government may ask people on this list to serve in the military. It is not necessary to be a citizen to register. If a man between the ages of eighteen and twenty-six comes to the United States to live, he must also register.

Everyone in the United States pays income tax. We pay taxes on the money we make. Taxes pay for our schools and roads, our police and firefighters. Income tax must be paid every year. April 15 is the last day you can send in federal income tax forms.

Ways to Participate in Democracy

Citizens can join a political party. They can also help with a campaign. They can even decide to run for office!

Citizens' ideas and opinions are important in a democracy. Citizens should give an elected official their opinion on an issue. They can call their senator or representative. They can write their opinion in a newspaper. They can publicly support or oppose an issue or policy.

Americans can join a civic group or a community group. There are groups to improve neighborhoods, parks, and schools.

5 CHECK YOUR UNDERSTANDING

Read the article. Write *T* for True or *F* for False. Then correct the false sentences.

_____ 1. New U.S. citizens give up their loyalty to other nations.

_____ 2. Only citizens can vote in federal elections.

_____ 3. Anyone can serve on a jury.

_____ 4. Only citizens register for the Selective Service.

_____ 5. Taxes pay for our schools and houses.

_____ 6. The last day you can send in a federal income tax form is April 16.

_____ 7. Immigrants who become citizens can run for office.

_____ 8. Elected officials want to know citizens' opinions.

6 READ AND WRITE

A READ. Go to page 175. Read sentences 55–56 aloud and check your pronunciation.

B WRITE. Go to page 177. Listen and write sentences 55–56.

7 CIVICS IN ACTION

DISCUSS. What civic groups are in the community where you live? Which groups would you want to join?

Connect to Your Active Book

Use e-flashcards to prepare for the civics test.

Do the record-and-compare exercises to prepare for the reading test.

Do the writing dictation exercises to prepare for the writing test.

Can you... answer the questions on page 111 about civic responsibilities? ☐

LESSON 1 U.S. BORDERS AND TERRITORIES

1 GET READY

A T058 🔊 **Listen to the questions. Do you know the answers?**

- Name <u>one</u> of the two longest rivers in the United States. (Question 88)
- What ocean is on the West Coast of the United States? (Question 89)
- What ocean is on the East Coast of the United States? (Question 90)
- Name <u>one</u> U.S. territory. (Question 91)
- Name <u>one</u> state that borders Canada. (Question 92)
- Name <u>one</u> state that borders Mexico. (Question 93)

B If you want to check your answers, go to pages 205 and 206.

2 WHAT DO YOU KNOW?

A Look at the map. Say the names of the countries and oceans.

B Look at the map on page 190. Use the compass on the map. What are two states in the East? in the West? in the North? in the South?

A Read the sentences. Do you know the words in bold?

1. The **residents** of Puerto Rico are called Puerto Ricans.
2. Mexico **borders** the United States.
3. Hawaii was a U.S. **territory** before it became a state.
4. There are many small **islands** in the Pacific Ocean.
5. California is on the West **Coast** of the United States.

B Match the words and the definitions.

_____ 1. to border
_____ 2. coast
_____ 3. island
_____ 4. resident
_____ 5. territory

a. land that is controlled by a particular country
b. be next to
c. the land next to the ocean
d. a piece of land surrounded by water
e. someone who lives in a particular place

4 **READ**

A T059 🔊 Listen and read the article.

B Read the article again. Write the words in the correct group.

American Samoa	Atlantic	Guam	Mississippi
Missouri	Northern Mariana Islands	Pacific	Puerto Rico
U.S. Virgin Islands			

U.S. territories   **Oceans**   **Rivers**

America, the Beautiful

The 50 States

The United States has fifty states. Forty-eight states are all connected together. Alaska and Hawaii are separate from the rest of the country. Hawaii is in the Pacific Ocean. Alaska borders the northwest coast of Canada.

U.S. Borders

The United States has two long coasts. The Pacific Ocean is on the West Coast of the United States. The Atlantic Ocean is on the East Coast of the United States. Canada and Mexico are the only two countries that border the United States.

Canada borders the United States on the north. The states of Maine, New Hampshire, Vermont, New York, Pennsylvania, Ohio, Michigan, Minnesota, North Dakota, Montana, Idaho, Washington, and Alaska border Canada.

Mexico borders the United States on the south. California, Arizona, New Mexico, and Texas are states that border Mexico.

U.S. Rivers

The Mississippi and Missouri are the longest rivers in the United States. They pass through thirty-one states. The Mississippi River is about 2,320 miles long. The Missouri River is 2,341 miles long.

U.S. Territories

The United States also has territories. These are lands that the United States controls, but they have some independence. U.S. territories in the Caribbean are Puerto Rico and the U.S. Virgin Islands. In the Pacific Ocean, U.S. territories are American Samoa, Northern Mariana Islands, and Guam. All of these U.S. territories are islands.

Alaska is the largest and most northern U.S. state.

The state of Hawaii is a group of islands in the Pacific Ocean.

Culture Note

Alaska became the 49th state in January, 1959. It has a longer coastline than all the other U.S. states combined. Hawaii became the 50th state in August, 1959. It is the only U.S. state made up entirely of islands.

5 CHECK YOUR UNDERSTANDING

Read the article again. Write the answers to the questions.

1. What are three states that border Canada?

   _____   _____   _____

2. What are three states that border Mexico?

   _____   _____   _____

3. What are the two longest rivers in the United States?

   _____   _____

4. What ocean is on the East Coast of the United States? _____

5. What ocean is on the West Coast of the United States? _____

6 READ AND WRITE

A READ. Go to page 175. Read sentences 57–58 aloud and check your pronunciation.

B WRITE. Go to page 177. Listen and write sentences 57–58.

7 CIVICS IN ACTION

DISCUSS. Look at the map on page 190. Find the state you live in. How does the location of your state affect the services your state government provides?

Connect to Your Active Book

Use e-flashcards to prepare for the civics test.

Do the record-and-compare exercises to prepare for the reading test.

Do the writing dictation exercises to prepare for the writing test.

Can you... answer the questions on page 115 about U.S. borders and territories? ☐

LESSON 1 THE STATUE OF LIBERTY

1 GET READY

A T060 🔊)) Listen to the question. Do you know the answer?

- Where is the Statue of Liberty? (Question 95)

B If you want to check your answer, go to page 206.

2 WHAT DO YOU KNOW?

Look at the picture. Millions of people visit the Statue of Liberty every year. Why do you think so many people come to see it?

Do you know the words in bold? What do the sentences mean? Circle *a* or *b*.

1. Many immigrants come to the United States because they want **liberty**.
   a. They want more freedom than they have at home.
   b. They want to find a political party.

2. The Statue of Liberty is a large statue of a woman **holding** a book and a light.
   a. The statue has a book and a light in her hands.
   b. The statue is on top of a book and a light.

3. The year 1876 was the 100-year **anniversary** of the Declaration of Independence.
   a. 1876 was the 100-year birthday of the Declaration of Independence.
   b. In 1876, the Declaration of Independence was written.

4. New York City has a large **harbor** where boats can stay safely.
   a. It has a large area of land for boats.
   b. It has a large area of water for boats.

5. New York City includes some **islands**.
   a. It has pieces of land surrounded by water.
   b. It has tall buildings.

4 READ

A T061 🔊 **Listen and read the article.**

B **Read the article again. Then complete the sentences. Use the words in the box.**

Declaration of Independence	New York harbor
Statue of Liberty	symbol

1. The French gave the Statue of Liberty to the United States to celebrate the 100-year anniversary of the _____.

2. The _____ is on Liberty Island.

3. It is the _____ of freedom.

4. The Statue of Liberty is in _____ .

The Lady of Liberty

The Statue of Liberty was a gift from the people of France to Americans to celebrate the 100-year anniversary of the Declaration of Independence. It is a giant statue of a woman. The woman is a symbol of liberty. She holds up a light to show people the way to freedom. She holds a book with the date July 4, 1776.

From 1892 to 1954, over 12 million immigrants entered the United States through New York harbor. They stayed on a small island that faced the Statue of Liberty. The immigrants had to wait days to have interviews and medical tests so they could enter the United States. As they waited to start a new life in America, they could see the statue. The Statue of Liberty became the symbol of freedom for immigrants coming to the United States.

Millions of people visit the Statue of Liberty every year. You can take a boat from New York City or from New Jersey to Liberty Island. Many people go there for a picnic or to walk up the 354 stairs to the head of the statue. There are 25 windows in the crown, and you can look out to see New York harbor.

Culture Note

"Give me your tired, your poor,
Your huddled masses yearning to breathe free,
The wretched refuse of your teeming shore.
Send these, the homeless, tempest-tossed to me,
I lift my lamp beside the golden door!"

These lines from a poem by Emma Lazarus can be found on the pedestal of the Statue.

Immigrants could see the Statue of Liberty as they waited in the immigration center.

5 CHECK YOUR UNDERSTANDING

Read the article. Write the answers to the questions.

1. Who gave the Statue of Liberty to the United States? _____

2. What does the Statue of Liberty celebrate? _____

3. Where is the Statue of Liberty? _____

4. How many immigrants came through New York between 1892 and 1954? _____

5. How do you get to the Statue of Liberty? _____

6. How many stairs are there to the top of the statue? _____

6 READ AND WRITE

A READ. **Go to page 175. Read sentences 59–60 aloud and check your pronunciation.**

B WRITE. **Go to page 177. Listen and write sentences 59–60.**

7 CIVICS IN ACTION

DISCUSS. **The Statue of Liberty is an important symbol. Make a list of other important symbols both in the United States and in your native country. Explain what they mean.**

Connect to Your Active Book

Use e-flashcards to prepare for the civics test.

Do the record-and-compare exercises to prepare for the reading test.

Do the writing dictation exercises to prepare for the writing test.

Can you... answer the question on page 119 about the Statue of Liberty? ☐

1 GET READY

A T062 🔊) **Listen to the questions. Do you know the answers?**

- What do we show loyalty to when we say the Pledge of Allegiance? (Question 52)
- Why does the flag have 13 stripes? (Question 96)
- Why does the flag have 50 stars? (Question 97)
- What is the name of the national anthem? (Question 98)

B If you want to check your answers, go to pages 204 and 206.

2 WHAT DO YOU KNOW?

Look at the pictures. Where is the American flag in each picture? Say the different ways the flag is used.

Saying the Pledge of Allegiance

A flag flying at half-staff

A U.S. federal building

Complete the sentences. Circle *a* or *b*.

1. A _____ is a fight between two armies in a war.
   a. battle
   b. treaty

2. A _____ is the official song of a nation that people sing at special events.
   a. symbol
   b. national anthem

3. The first thirteen colonies were the _____ states.
   a. final
   b. original

4. When people put the American flag outside their home, they show their _____ to the United States.
   a. loyalty
   b. citizenship

5. A _____ is an official promise you make.
   a. pledge
   b. responsibility

4 **READ**

T063
A ◄))) **Listen and read the article.**

B **Read the article again. Then complete the sentences. Use the words in the box.**

blue	colonies	Pledge of Allegiance	red
star	stripes	"The Star-Spangled Banner"	white

1. The colors of the American flag are _____ , _____ , and _____ .

2. The thirteen stripes in the flag represent the thirteen original _____ .

3. There is a _____ on the flag for each state.

4. The national anthem is _____ .

5. People say the _____ to show their loyalty to the United States.

The Land of the Free and the Home of the Brave

Stars and Stripes

The colors of the American flag are red, white, and blue. The American flag has thirteen stripes to represent the original thirteen colonies. These thirteen colonies declared independence from England in 1776 and created the United States of America.

In the first flag, there were also thirteen stars because there were thirteen original states. As the country grew, it added a star for each state. There are now fifty states in the United States. So there are now fifty stars on the flag. Each star represents a state. The last star was added when Hawaii became a state in 1959.

The original flag had thirteen stars.

The National Anthem

The name of the U.S. national anthem is "The Star-Spangled Banner." It is a song about the American flag and a battle between England and the United States. In 1812, the English attacked an American fort. A man, Francis Scott Key, was watching the battle through the night. In the morning, he saw that the American flag was still there and knew the Americans had won the battle.

The Pledge of Allegiance

The flag represents the United States of America. People show their loyalty to the United States and to the American flag when they say the Pledge of Allegiance. Many children say the Pledge of Allegiance every morning in school.

THE PLEDGE OF ALLEGIANCE

I pledge allegiance

to the flag

of the United States of America,

and to the republic

for which it stands, one nation

under God, indivisible

with liberty and justice for all.

Culture Note

When people sing the National Anthem or say the Pledge of Allegiance, they face the flag, take their hats off, and usually put their right hand over their heart.

Read the article. Complete the sentences. Circle *a* or *b*.

1. There are fifty _____ in the flag because there are fifty states.
   a. stars   **b.** stripes

2. The flag has three _____.
   a. colors   **b.** stars

3. The thirteen stripes represent the thirteen _____.
   a. flags   **b.** colonies

4. School children often say _____ at the beginning of their day.
   a. the Pledge of Allegiance   **b.** "The Star-Spangled Banner"

5. People sing _____ at special events.
   a. the Pledge of Allegiance   **b.** "The Star-Spangled Banner"

6. _____ is the national anthem.
   a. The Pledge of Allegiance   **b.** "The Star-Spangled Banner"

6 **READ AND WRITE**

A **READ.** Go to page 175. Read sentences 61–62 aloud and check your pronunciation.

B **WRITE.** Go to page 177. Listen and write sentences 61–62.

7 **CIVICS IN ACTION**

DISCUSS. Think about places where you have seen the American flag. Why or how was it being used in each place?

Connect to Your Active Book

Use e-flashcards to prepare for the civics test.

Do the record-and-compare exercises to prepare for the reading test.

Do the writing dictation exercises to prepare for the writing test.

Can you… answer the questions on page 123 about the American flag? ☐

1 GET READY

A T064 🔊) **Listen to the questions. Do you know the answers?**

- When do we celebrate Independence Day? (Question 99)
- Name <u>two</u> national U.S. holidays. (Question 100)

B If you want to check your answers, go to page 206.

2 WHAT DO YOU KNOW?

Look at the pictures. Write the words from the box below each picture.

barbecue	fireworks	parade

1. _____ 2. _____ 3. _____

A Read the sentences. Do you know the words in bold?

1. Americans **celebrate** ten national holidays.

2. Some holidays **honor** important people in U.S. history.

3. Fireworks are an Independence Day **tradition**.

4. More than 22 million Americans are **veterans** of U.S. wars.

5. On **Memorial** Day people remember soldiers who died in war.

B Match the words and the definitions.

_____ 1. celebrate   **a.** something that people have done for a long time

_____ 2. honor   **b.** remembering people who have died

_____ 3. memorial   **c.** to show respect to someone or something important

_____ 4. tradition   **d.** someone who has been a soldier in war

_____ 5. veteran   **e.** to do something special because it is an important day

4 READ

A T065 🔊 Listen and read the article.

B Read the article again. Then write the month for each holiday.

_____ 1. New Year's Day

_____ 2. Martin Luther King, Jr. Day

_____ 3. Presidents' Day

_____ 4. Memorial Day

_____ 5. Flag Day

_____ 6. Independence Day

_____ 7. Labor Day

_____ 8. Columbus Day

_____ 9. Veterans Day

_____ 10. Thanksgiving

_____ 11. Christmas

Days to Celebrate

Culture Note

On June 14, 1777, the colonies decided to make their first national flag. Flag Day is on June 14. It is not a national holiday.

New Year's Day

In the United States, people begin to celebrate the new year on December 31, New Year's Eve. Many people go to big parties. At midnight, they say, "Happy New Year" and kiss one another. Some people make resolutions, or promises, for the new year.

Martin Luther King, Jr. Day

This holiday honors the leader of the Civil Rights Movement (see page 49). People remember Dr. King and promise to continue his work for equality. MLK Day is celebrated on the third Monday of January.

Presidents' Day

This holiday celebrates the birthday of two important U.S. presidents: George Washington and Abraham Lincoln (see pages 21 and 33). Presidents' Day is on the third Monday of February.

Memorial Day

On this day, people remember the military men and women who died in wars. Americans say Memorial Day marks the beginning of the summer. Memorial Day is celebrated on the last Monday of May.

Independence Day

This holiday celebrates the signing of the Declaration of Independence (see page 13). People usually have picnics, go to parades, and watch fireworks at night. Independence Day is on July 4.

Labor Day

This holiday honors working people. Americans usually celebrate the holiday with picnics and barbecues. Labor Day marks the end of summer. It is on the first Monday of September.

Columbus Day

On this day, we remember the history of America. Columbus Day celebrates Christopher Columbus's arrival in the Americas on October 12, 1492. Columbus Day is on the second Monday of October.

Veterans Day

This day honors all the men and women who have served in the U.S. military. People often go to parades. Veterans Day is always celebrated on November 11.

Thanksgiving

This is a day to give thanks. Pilgrims and Native Americans celebrated the first Thanksgiving in 1621 (see page 5). The tradition is to have a turkey dinner on this day. Thanksgiving is celebrated on the fourth Thursday of November.

Christmas

Christmas is on December 25. It celebrates the birth of Jesus Christ. Some families get together to exchange gifts.

5 CHECK YOUR UNDERSTANDING

Read the article. Match the holidays with the descriptions.

_____ 1. New Year's Day

_____ 2. Martin Luther King, Jr. Day

_____ 3. Presidents' Day

_____ 4. Memorial Day

_____ 5. Independence Day

_____ 6. Labor Day

_____ 7. Veterans Day

_____ 8. Thanksgiving

_____ 9. Christmas

a. is on July 4.

b. honors working people.

c. celebrates Lincoln's and Washington's birthdays.

d. is a Christian holiday.

e. is celebrated with a turkey dinner.

f. celebrates a civil rights leader.

g. honors all the people who serve in the U.S. military.

h. remembers soldiers who died in wars.

i. is celebrated with a big party at midnight.

6 READ AND WRITE

A READ. **Go to page 175. Read sentences 63–64 aloud and check your pronunciation.**

B WRITE. **Go to page 177. Listen and write sentences 63–64.**

7 CIVICS IN ACTION

DISCUSS. **What is your favorite American holiday? Describe how you celebrate this holiday.**

Connect to Your Active Book

Use e-flashcards to prepare for the civics test.

Do the record-and-compare exercises to prepare for the reading test.

Do the writing dictation exercises to prepare for the writing test.

Can you... answer the questions on page 127 about holidays in the United States? ☐

OVERVIEW

During your interview, the officer will assess your ability to speak English. This speaking test begins in the waiting room when the officer greets you and lasts through the interview. To pass the test, you must speak English in a way that can be understood by the officer. To see the USCIS scoring guidelines for the Speaking section of the English Test, go to the official website of United States Citizenship and Immigration Services at www.uscis.gov or click on the Resources tab at the bottom of each Active Book screen.

FUTURE U.S. CITIZENS: THE STUDENT BOOK

Part 2 Speaking Test Prep contains four units with 22 lessons. Unit 1 will help you understand and use the grammar you will need for the interview. Unit 2 will help you follow directions and use appropriate body language. Units 3 and 4 will help you use speaking strategies, such as making small talk and asking for clarification, and will also help you practice your pronunciation. Three model interviews with applicants illustrate the grammar, speaking strategies, and pronunciation points. Each lesson ends with a role play so you can practice speaking and feel more confident at your interview. For many role plays, you need to use your N-400 application. You can bring a copy of your real application to class. If you are not comfortable using real information, you can fill out an N-400 with made-up information just to use for the role plays.

FUTURE U.S. CITIZENS: THE ACTIVE BOOK

Use the *Future U.S. Citizens* Active Book to help you study.

- The entire book is in digital form on the Active Book, so you can read and listen to the speaking lessons on a computer. When you see ◀)), click on it to play audio files. When you see ◼◀, click on it to play segments of the videos.

- You can also watch each of the videos in full by going to the bottom of the screen and clicking on the Video tab. Watching the full videos will help you feel more comfortable at your interview.

LESSON 1 YES/NO QUESTIONS AND SHORT ANSWERS

Yes/No questions with be	Short answers	
Are you willing to take the Oath of Allegiance?	Yes, I am.	No, I'm not.
Is your husband a U.S. citizen?	Yes, he is.	No, he isn't.
Were you ever married before?	Yes, I was.	No, I wasn't.
Was your daughter born here?	Yes, she was.	No, she wasn't.

Grammar Watch

Do not use contractions with affirmative short answers. For example, do not say *Yes, I'm.* Say *Yes, I am.*

1 PRACTICE

A V2 S1 Watch the video. Weimin Gao is at his naturalization interview. What does the officer ask? Circle *a* or *b*.

    a. Are you willing to take the Oath of Allegiance, Mr. Gao?

    b. Are you ready to take the Oath of Allegiance, Mr. Gao?

B V2 S1 Watch the video again. What does Mr. Gao say? Circle *a* or *b*.

    a. Yes, I am.   **b.** No, I'm not.

C Read the questions an officer may ask an applicant. Answer the questions. Use short answers.

    1. A: Are your parents in the United States?

        B: Yes, _____.

    2. A: Is your husband from Mexico?

        B: No, _____.

    3. A: Were your children born in Peru?

        B: No, _____.

    4. A: Was your wife married before?

        B: No, _____.

    5. A: Are you still at the same address?

        B: Yes, _____.

Yes/No questions with *do* and *did*	Short answers	
Do you have any other phone numbers?	Yes, I do.	No, I don't.
Does your wife live with you?	Yes, she does.	No, she doesn't.
Did you travel outside of the United States?	Yes, I did.	No, I didn't.
Did any of those trips last more than six months?	Yes, they did.	No, they didn't.

2 PRACTICE

A Read the questions an officer may ask an applicant. Answer the questions. Use short answers.

1. Do you want to change your name? Yes, _____ .

2. Did you bring your permanent resident card? Yes, _____ .

3. Do you live at 320 Carpenter Avenue? Yes, _____ .

4. Do you have any children? No, _____ .

5. Did you have any trouble finding our office? No, _____ .

B Complete the conversations between an officer and an applicant. Use short answers.

1. **A:** Are you Mr. Park?

   B: Yes, _____ .

   A: Good morning. I'm Ms. Carter. Did you have any trouble finding parking?

   B: No, _____ . I found a spot nearby.

   A: That's good. Now you do understand what we're going to do today?

   B: Yes, _____ .

   A: Now please raise your right hand. Do you swear to tell the truth during this interview?

   B: Yes, _____ .

2. **A:** OK, Mr. Park. Are you still at 450 Encino Boulevard?

   B: Yes, _____ .

   A: Are you married?

   B: Yes, _____ .

   A: Does your wife live with you?

   B: Yes, _____ .

Show what you know!

ROLE-PLAY. PAIRS. Practice the conversations in Exercises 1C and 2B. Take turns being the officer and the applicant.

LESSON 2 TAG QUESTIONS

Negative tag questions	Answers that show agreement	
Traffic is bad today, **isn't it?**	Yes, **it is.**	It sure **is.**
The wind last night was awful, **wasn't it?**	Yes, **it was.**	Yes, **it was** terrible.
There were a lot of delays today, **weren't there?**	Yes, **there were.**	Yes, the buses **were** late.
It looks like rain today, **doesn't it?**	Yes, **it does.**	Yes, **it's** really cloudy.
Weekends seem to fly by, **don't they?**	Yes, **they do**.	Yes, **they** really **do**.

Grammar Watch

A tag question is a statement + a short *yes/no* question. If the statement is affirmative, the tag question is negative. We can use tag questions to make small talk, which is light, friendly conversation. During the naturalization interview, the officer may use tag questions to make small talk.

1 PRACTICE

Pronunciation Watch

You can use a tag question when you expect the other person to agree with you. In this type of tag question, the voice falls at the end of the tag.

V1 S1

A ◼️◀ Watch the video. Maria Rivas is at her naturalization interview. Which question does the officer ask her? Circle *a* or *b*.

    a. It's very cold today, isn't it?   **b.** It's a beautiful day, isn't it?

B Read the questions an officer may use to make small talk. Complete the conversations.

    1. A: It's really hot today, _____ it?

        B: Yes, _____ .

    2. A: The buses were really crowded today, _____ they?

        B: Yes, _____ .

    3. A: It feels really cold out today, _____ it?

        B: Yes, _____ .

    4. A: Traffic was terrible this morning, _____ it?

        B: Yes, _____ .

    5. A: There were a lot of people in the waiting room, _____ there?

        B: Yes, _____ .

Affirmative tag questions	Answers that show agreement	
It isn't very hot out this morning, **is it?**	No, **it isn't.**	No, **it's** actually cool.
Traffic wasn't bad this afternoon, **was it?**	No, **it wasn't.**	No, in fact **it was** very light.
There wasn't much traffic today, **was there?**	No, **there wasn't.**	No, **there** really **wasn't.**
The air conditioning doesn't seem to be on, **does it?**	No, **it doesn't.**	No, **it's** very warm in here.
It didn't rain much at all this morning, **did it?**	No, **it didn't.**	No, **it** just **drizzled.**

2 PRACTICE

Read the questions an officer may use to confirm information. Complete the conversations.

Grammar Watch

In affirmative tag questions, the statement is negative and the tag is affirmative. If you agree with the statement, your answer is *no*.

1. **A:** You aren't cold, _____?

   B: No, _____.

2. **A:** There wasn't much traffic this afternoon, _____?

   B: No, _____.

Pronunciation Watch

You can use a tag question to confirm information. In this type of tag question, the voice goes up and then falls at the end of the tag.

3. **A:** It isn't raining out now, _____?

   B: No, _____.

4. **A:** We didn't get much snow this morning, _____?

   B: No, _____.

5. **A:** You didn't wait too long in the waiting room, _____?

   B: No, _____.

6. **A:** It didn't take a long time to get through security, _____?

   B: No, _____.

Show what you know!

ROLE-PLAY. PAIRS. Practice the conversations in Exercises 1B and 2. Take turns being the officer and the applicant.

LESSON 3 YES/NO QUESTIONS IN THE PRESENT PERFECT

Yes/no questions in the present perfect	Short answers
Have you traveled outside of the United States in the past five years?	Yes, I have. No, I haven't.
Has your husband been married before?	Yes, he has. No, he hasn't.

Yes/no questions in the present perfect	Long answers
Have you ever taken any trips to your country?	Yes. I've taken two trips home. No. I haven't been there since I left.
Has your husband ever been married before?	Yes. He was married once before. No. He's never been married before.

Grammar Watch

You can use questions with *ever* to find out if someone has done something one time or more.
Do not use contractions in affirmative short answers with the present perfect. For example, do not say *Yes, I've.* Say *Yes, I have.*

1 PRACTICE

A **V3 S1** Watch the video. The officer asks Ekaterina Andropova about claiming to be a citizen. How does she answer? Circle *a* or *b*.

   a. Yes, I have.   **b.** No, I haven't.

B Read the questions an officer may ask an applicant. Choose the correct short answer. Circle *a* or *b*.

1. Have you ever claimed to be a U.S. citizen?
      a. No, I haven't.   **b.** No, I hadn't.

2. Have you always done the same kind of work?
      a. Yes, I have work.   **b.** Yes, I have.

3. Have you taken any trips longer than six months?
      a. No, I didn't.   **b.** No, I haven't.

4. Have you ever been a member of a terrorist organization?
      a. No, I haven't.   **b.** No, I wasn't.

5. Have you always paid your taxes on time?
      a. Yes, I have.   **b.** Yes, I have paid.

A Complete the sentences with the present perfect. Use the verbs in parentheses.
Use contractions when possible.

1. I _____ _____ two trips outside of the United States since getting my green card. *(take)*

2. My husband _____ _____ married twice. *(be)*

3. I _____ never _____ anyone that I was a U.S. citizen. *(tell)*

4. We _____ always _____ our taxes on time. *(pay)*

5. My children _____ always _____ with me. *(live)*

B Read the questions an officer may ask an applicant. Complete the conversations.
Use the verbs in parentheses. Use contractions when possible.

1. **A:** Have you _____ your passport? *(bring)*

   B: Yes, I _____. Here it is.

2. **A:** Has your family _____ outside of the United States? *(travel)*

   B: Yes. We _____ _____ to Ecuador two times.

3. **A:** Have you ever _____ in the U.S. armed forces? *(serve)*

   B: No, I _____ never _____ in the armed forces.

4. **A:** Have your parents _____ to live in the United States? *(come)*

   B: No, they _____.

5. **A:** Have you ever _____ your home country? *(visit)*

   B: Yes. I _____ _____ my family two times.

6. **A:** Has your wife ever been _____ *(marry)*

   B: Yes. She _____ _____ once before.

Show what you know!

ROLE-PLAY. PAIRS. Practice the conversations in Exercises 1B and 2B. Take turns being the officer and the applicant.

LESSON 4 HOW LONG AND HOW MANY
WITH PRESENT PERFECT

How long and How many with present perfect	Answers
How many times have you been married?	Twice. I've been married twice.
How long have you worked for that doctor?	For seven years. I've worked for him for seven years.

Grammar Watch

You can use *How long* with the simple past.

A: *How long did you work at the restaurant?*   A: *How long did you work at the school?*
B: *I worked there for six years.*   B: *For five years.*

1 PRACTICE

A V2 S2   Watch the video. What question does the officer ask Mr. Gao? Circle *a* or *b*.

    a. How long have you lived at your current address?

    b. How long have you been at this address?

B Read the questions an officer may ask an applicant. Circle the correct answer.

    1. **How long / How many** have you lived at this address?

    2. **How long / How many** times have you traveled to Brazil?

    3. **How long / How many** have you worked at this company?

    4. **How long / How many** trips have you taken to your country?

C Read the questions an officer may ask an applicant. Match the answers. Write the letter.

    _____ 1. How long have you had your new job?   a. I've been married for ten years.

    _____ 2. How long have you been married?   b. I've had it for six months.

    _____ 3. How many years have you been in Dallas?   c. I waited a year.

    _____ 4. How long did you wait for your interview?   d. I've been here for eight years.

Complete the conversations between an officer and an applicant. Use *How long,*
How many, **and the verbs in parentheses. Use contractions when possible.**

1. **A:** So, Mrs. Han, I'm going to ask you a few questions. _____
   _____ have you lived at 789 Sycamore Street?

   B: I _____ _____ there for two years. (*live*)

2. **A:** _____ _____ times have you changed addresses?

   B: Let me think. I _____ _____ three times. (*move*)

3. **A:** And tell me about your job. _____ _____ have you
   worked at the supermarket?

   B: I _____ _____ there for eight years. (*work*)

4. **A:** _____ _____ have you been a manager there?

   B: For one year.

5. **A:** OK. And _____ _____ times have you been
   promoted?

   B: Two times. The first time I became a shift manager and then a store manager.

6. **A:** _____ _____ trips have you taken outside of the
   United States?

   B: Four. I _____ _____ four trips to my country. (*take*)

7. **A:** And _____ _____ days did each trip last?

   B: Two trips were for two weeks. One was for three weeks. One lasted a month.

8. **A:** Mrs. Han, you say you are a member of a business association.
   _____ _____ have you been a member?

   B: I _____ _____ a member for four years. (*be*)

Show what you know!

ROLE-PLAY. PAIRS. Practice the conversations in Exercises 1C and 2. Take turns
being the officer and the applicant.

LESSON 1 GREETINGS AND SHAKING HANDS

1 BEFORE YOU WATCH

A Look at the picture. Ms. Andropova is in the waiting room at the USCIS office. The Immigration Services Officer is Manuel Vega. Describe what is happening.

B **PREDICT.** Check (✓) the things you think the officer will say. Then compare your answers with a partner.

☐ **1.** Are you Ms. Andropova?

☐ **2.** I am Manuel Vega.

☐ **3.** Why are you here?

☐ **4.** I am a USCIS Immigration Services officer.

☐ **5.** Do you want to shake hands?

☐ **6.** What time is your interview?

2 WATCH

A V3 S2 🔲◀ Read the sentences in Exercise 1B again. Watch the video. Write a star (★) next to the sentences you hear.

B V3 S2 🔲◀ Watch the video again. Answer the questions. Circle *a* or *b*.

1. How does Ms. Andropova greet the officer?
   a. Good morning.   **b.** Good afternoon.

2. What does Ms. Andropova say?
   a. Pleased to meet you.   **b.** Nice to meet you.

3 INTERVIEW STRATEGY Greetings and shaking hands

A READ. **Underline any information that you did not know.**

When you meet the officer, it is important to greet him or her appropriately. This helps you to make a good impression.

- Stand up, smile, and make eye contact when the officer calls your name. Confirm your name. You can say *That's me* or *Yes, I'm* _______.
- Greet the officer. You can say *Hello, Good morning,* or *Good afternoon.*
- Shake hands with the officer. Use your right hand. In the United States, people shake hands for three to five seconds with a firm handshake. When you shake hands, remember to make eye contact and smile.
- Ask the officer to repeat his or her name if you did not hear or understand it.

B **Do people shake hands in your country when they meet for the first time? Do men and women shake hands?**

C V3 S2 **Watch the video again. Check (✓) the true statements about Ms. Andropova.**

☐ **1.** She stood up.

☐ **2.** She told the officer her name.

☐ **3.** She made eye contact.

☐ **4.** She did not shake the officer's hand.

☐ **5.** She smiled.

☐ **6.** She asked the officer the time.

☐ **7.** She asked the officer to repeat his name.

Culture Note

In some cultures, men and women do not shake hands. In the United States, people shake hands when they meet for the first time and in business or formal situations.

Show what you know!

ROLE-PLAY. PAIRS. **Student A, you are the officer. Introduce yourself and greet the applicant. Student B, you are the applicant. Greet the officer and shake hands.**

Can you... greet someone and shake hands? ☐

1 BEFORE YOU WATCH

A **READ.** Underline any information that you did not know.

> After the officer calls your name and greets you, he or she may make small talk, or light conversation. People often make small talk to help someone feel comfortable in a new situation. Small talk topics usually include the weather, traffic, a sports event, or other friendly topics. Small talk topics are not serious, such as personal, political, or religious topics.

B **PREDICT.** Check (✓) the topics you think the officer may talk about when you meet. Then compare your answers with a partner.

☐ **1.** the weather

☐ **2.** politics

☐ **3.** the citizenship test

☐ **4.** popular music

☐ **5.** finding the USCIS office

☐ **6.** sports

☐ **7.** traffic

☐ **8.** length of time in the waiting room

2 WATCH

A V3 S3 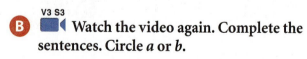 Read the topics in Exercise 1B again. Watch the video. Write a star (★) next to the topics the officer and Ms. Andropova talk about.

B V3 S3 Watch the video again. Complete the sentences. Circle *a* or *b*.

1. The officer is in a good mood because _____ .
   a. the weather is nice
   b. it is Friday

2. Ms. Andropova did not have trouble finding the office because _____ .
   a. she has been to the office before
   b. she works near the USCIS office

3. The officer says the weather in Houston _____.
   a. is too rainy all the time
   b. is dry for a long time and then it rains too much

A **READ.** Underline any information that you did not know.

> When the officer makes small talk, you can show you are listening by smiling when it is appropriate and nodding your head to show that you understand. Make sure your answers are short; do not give many details or tell a long story.

B **V3 S3** Watch the video again. Check (✓) the true statements about Ms. Andropova.

☐ 1. She talks too much.

☐ 2. She only talks about appropriate topics.

☐ 3. She changes the topic.

☐ 4. She asks the officer a personal question.

C Do people make small talk in your country? Describe situations and topics that are acceptable.

Situations	Acceptable Topics

Show what you know!

ROLE-PLAY. PAIRS. Student A, you are the officer. Introduce yourself and make small talk. Student B, you are the applicant. Practice making small talk.

Can you...make small talk? ☐

LESSON 3 USING POLITE LANGUAGE AND FOLLOWING DIRECTIONS

1 BEFORE YOU WATCH

A **READ.** Underline any information that you did not know.

> It is important to demonstrate polite behavior from the start of your naturalization interview. The officer will greet you politely and then ask you to come to the office. If you have a coat or umbrella, you can ask where to place them. In English, some polite expressions include *excuse me, could you, may I, please,* and *thank you.*

B **PREDICT.** Look at the picture. Check (✓) what you think the officer will say. Then compare your answers with a partner.

☐ **1.** Tell me your name.

☐ **2.** Please come in.

☐ **3.** Would you like to hang up your coat?

☐ **4.** Are you ready to take an oath?

☐ **5.** Can you raise your right hand?

☐ **6.** Please have a seat.

2 WATCH

A V3 S4 🔲◀ Read the sentences in Exercise 1B again. Watch the video. Write a star (★) next to the sentences you hear.

B V3 S4 🔲◀ Watch the video again. Put the sentences about Ms. Andropova in order. Write *1, 2, 3, 4, 5, 6.*

_____ **a.** She sits down.

_____ **b.** She asks about her umbrella.

_____ **c.** She hangs up her coat.

_1_ **d.** She follows the officer into the room.

_____ **e.** She puts her umbrella next to the door.

_____ **f.** She takes an oath to tell the truth.

A **READ.** Underline any information that you did not know.

During the naturalization interview, it is important to be polite and follow directions. Pay attention to what the officer asks you or tells you to do.

- In the waiting room, the officer may say *Please follow me*. Let the officer walk first; then follow.

- In the office, the officer may say *Have a seat* or *Please sit down*. Then sit down. It is appropriate to say *Thank you* as you sit down.

- The officer may say *Would you like to hang up your coat?* You can answer *Yes, thank you* and wait for his or her response.

B Read the sentences an officer may say. Which is more polite? Circle *a* or *b*.

1. **a.** Come in now.   **b.** Please come in.
2. **a.** Sit down.   **b.** Have a seat.
3. **a.** Where may I put my umbrella?   **b.** Where does my umbrella go?
4. **a.** Thank you.   **b.** Thanks.
5. **a.** Hang your coat on the door.   **b.** You may hang your coat on the door.
6. **a.** Please follow me.   **b.** Come this way.

C **PAIRS.** Change each conversation to make it more polite. Then practice the new conversations.

1. **A:** Come in.   **A:** _____
   B: Thanks.   **B:** _____

2. **A:** Hang your coat there.   **A:** _____
   B: OK.   **B:** _____

Show what you know!

ROLE-PLAY. PAIRS. Student A, you are the officer. Invite the applicant to come into your office, hang up his or her coat, and have a seat.
Student B, you are the applicant. Use polite language and follow directions.

Can you... use polite language and follow directions? ☐

LESSON 4 USING APPROPRIATE BODY LANGUAGE

1 BEFORE YOU WATCH

A READ. Underline any information that you did not know.

> After you swear to tell the truth, the officer will ask to see your passport, your permanent resident card, your photos, and sometimes other documents. The officer may ask you to confirm that you know the purpose of your naturalization interview.

B What is the purpose of the naturalization interview? Write your ideas.

_____

_____

_____

_____

_____

2 WATCH

V3 S5

A ◀ Watch the video. Are the sentences below true or false? Write *T* for True or *F* for False.

_____ **1.** The officer asks to see Ms. Andropova's driver's license.

_____ **2.** Ms. Andropova understands what they are going to do in the interview.

_____ **3.** The officer asks Ms. Andropova if she is ready to become a U.S. citizen.

_____ **4.** She doesn't think she is ready to become a citizen.

V3 S5

B ◀ Watch the video again. Why does Ms. Andropova want to become a U.S. citizen? Complete the sentences.

_____ I _____ this country.

It means _____ to me. America means to me

_____ to pursue my dreams.

A READ. **Underline any information that you did not know.**

> During the naturalization interview, it is important to use appropriate body language. This helps you to make a good impression.
>
> • Make eye contact when the officer speaks to you or when you answer a question. In the United States, making eye contact shows that you are listening and telling the truth.
>
> • Sit up straight during the interview. This shows the officer that you are paying attention.
>
> • You can use your hands to gesture while you speak, but generally keep your hands on your lap during the interview.
>
> • Keep your feet on the floor. Don't cross your legs.

V3 S6

B Watch the video. Check (✓) the true statements about Ms. Andropova's body language.

☐ 1. She sits up straight when listening to the questions.

☐ 2. She has her hands on the desk.

☐ 3. She seems interested in the questions.

☐ 4. She looks the officer in the eyes.

☐ 5. She crosses her legs.

C What are some things you should <u>not</u> do during your interview? For example, don't chew gum.

D What is appropriate body language for a formal interview in your native country? Is it similar to or different from appropriate body language in an interview in the United States?

Show what you know!

ROLE-PLAY. PAIRS. **Student A, you are the officer. Ask the applicant for his or her documents. Then ask why he or she wants to become an American citizen.**
Student B, you are the applicant. Give your documents to the officer. Answer his or her questions. Use appropriate body language.

Can you. . .use appropriate body language? ☐

LESSON 1 ASKING FOR REPETITION

1 BEFORE YOU WATCH

A Go to page 180. Look at Part 1 of the N-400 Application and the glossed words. This section asks about your legal name (your name as it appears on your Permanent Resident Card). It asks if you want to change your name.

B The officer will ask you to confirm your name and if you want to change your name. What are some possible questions?

_____

_____

_____

_____

2 WATCH

A V1 S2  Watch the video. What information does the officer say he is going to verify? Circle *a*, *b*, or *c*.

a. personal information

b. financial information

c. physical information

B V1 S2 Watch the video again. Write *T* for True or *F* for False.

_____ **1.** Mrs. Rivas's full legal name is Maria Rivas.

_____ **2.** Her maiden name is Martha.

_____ **3.** Mrs. Rivas wants to keep her name.

3 SPEAKING STRATEGY   Asking for repetition

If you do not understand the officer's question or request, do not try to guess what the officer said. It's fine to ask the officer to repeat the question or the request. You can say *Could you repeat that, please?* or *Could you say that again?*

A T066 🔊 **Listen to part of Mrs. Rivas's naturalization interview. What does she ask the officer? Circle *a* or *b*.**

a. Could you say that more slowly, Mr. Peterson?

b. Could you repeat that, Mr. Peterson?

B **Here are ways to ask someone to repeat something.**

Could you repeat that, please?

Could you say that again?

Excuse me, can you say that again?

I'm sorry, can you please repeat that?

4 PRONUNCIATION

Pronunciation Watch

Can you, Could you

In questions, *can you* is often pronounced "k'nya ."
Could you is often pronounced "couldja."

T067
🔊 **Listen and repeat.**

I'm sorry. Could you repeat that, please?   Can you say that again, please?

Could you say that again?   Can you please repeat that?

Show what you know!

ROLE-PLAY. PAIRS. Look at your own N-400 Application. Give Part 1 to your partner. Student A, you are the officer. Ask questions about your partner's legal name and if he or she wants to change names.
Student B, you are the applicant. Ask the officer to repeat the questions.

Can you... ask someone to repeat? ☐

1 **BEFORE YOU WATCH**

A Go to page 181. Look at Parts 3 and 4 of the N-400 Application and the glossed words. This section asks about personal information, for example, your date of birth, your marital status, address, telephone numbers, and more.

B The officer may ask you to confirm your address and to check if your telephone numbers are still the same. What are some possible questions?

_____

_____

_____

_____

2 **WATCH**

A V1 S3
🎬 Watch the video. The officer notices a mistake on Mrs. Rivas's N-400 form. What is it?

B V1 S3
🎬 Watch the video again. Answer the questions. Circle *a*, *b*, or *c*.

1. What year was Mrs. Rivas born?
   a. 1971   **b.** 1973   **c.** 1974

2. Where is Mrs. Rivas from?
   a. El Salvador   **b.** Mexico   **c.** Guatemala

3. What is Mrs. Rivas's marital status?
   a. widowed   **b.** divorced   **c.** married

4. Where does Mrs. Rivas live now?
   a. Los Alamos   **b.** Los Angeles   **c.** Long Beach

5. Which telephone number does Mrs. Rivas have on her form?
   a. home phone   **b.** cell phone   **c.** home and cell phones

SPEAKING STRATEGY Checking your understanding

> During the interview, if it is not clear what the officer is asking
> you, check your understanding before you answer. Say in your
> own words what you have understood, for example, *My address.*
> *Do you mean where I live?*

A T068 🔊)) Listen to part of Mrs. Rivas's naturalization interview. What does she say
to check her understanding? Circle *a* or *b*.

1. a. You mean my birthday?   **b.** Do you mean my birthday?

2. a. My marital status means if I'm married?   **b.** My marital status means is my
husband married?

B Here are ways to check your understanding.

You mean . . . ?

Do you mean . . . ?

Does that mean . . . ?

4 **PRONUNCIATION**

Pronunciation Watch

Intonation of *Yes/No* Questions	**Intonation of statements as questions**
When we ask a *Yes/No* question, our voice goes up at the end. This is called rising intonation.	We can use rising intonation with a statement to ask a question.

T069
🔊)) **Listen and repeat.**

Can you please tell me your date of birth?   My birthday?

Do you have any other phone numbers?   The phone number at my house?

Show what you know!

ROLE-PLAY. PAIRS. Look at your own N-400 Application. Give Parts 3 and 4 to
your partner. Student A, you are the officer. Ask questions about your partner's
marital status and current address(es) and phone number(s).
Student B, you are the applicant. Check your understanding of Student A's questions.

Can you...check your understanding of questions? ☐

LESSON 3 ASKING SOMEONE TO SPEAK MORE SLOWLY OR LOUDER

1 BEFORE YOU WATCH

A Go to page 182. Look at Part 6 of the N-400 Application and the glossed words. This section asks about your residence and employment.

B The officer may ask you about your current and past jobs. What are some possible questions?

_____

_____

_____

2 WATCH

A V1 S4 Watch the video. Does Mrs. Rivas have a job now?

B V1 S4 Watch the video again. Answer the questions. Circle *a* or *b*.

1. What is Mrs. Rivas's current place of employment?
   a. a school
   b. a doctor's office

2. What does she do at her current job?
   a. She is a receptionist.
   b. She is a doctor.

3. How long has she worked at her current job?
   a. Two months
   b. Two years

4. What was her job before?
   a. She was a teacher's aide.
   b. She worked at a school cafeteria.

5. Why did she change jobs?
   a. The new job pays more.
   b. The new job has better hours.

SPEAKING STRATEGY Ask someone to speak more slowly or louder

> The officer might speak very fast during the interview or have an accent that you are not familiar with. If you would like the officer to speak more slowly, you can say *Could you please speak more slowly?* If you did not hear a question, you can say *Excuse me, I didn't hear you. Could you please say that louder?*

A T070 🔊 **Listen to part of Mrs. Rivas's naturalization interview. What does she ask the officer? Circle *a* or *b*.**

a. Could you say that more slowly?   **b.** Could you speak more slowly?

B **Here are ways to ask someone to speak more slowly or louder.**

Could you please speak more slowly?

Could you say that more slowly, please?

Excuse me, I didn't hear you. Could you please say that louder?

I'm sorry, I couldn't hear the question. Can you please speak louder?

4 **PRONUNCIATION**

Pronunciation Watch

Sentence stress

In conversation, we stress the most important words. This means that we say them in a louder, stronger voice.

T071
🔊 **Listen and repeat.**

• •
I'm sorry. I couldn't hear you.

• • •
Can you please speak louder? I didn't hear the question.

Show what you know!

**ROLE-PLAY. PAIRS. Look at your own N-400 application. Give Part 6 to your partner. Student A, you are the officer. Ask questions about the applicant's residence and employment.
Student B, you are the applicant. Ask the officer to speak more slowly or louder.**

Can you...ask someone to speak more slowly or louder? ☐

1 | BEFORE YOU WATCH

Go to page 183. Look at Part 7 of the N-400 Application and the glossed words. This section asks about time you may have spent outside the United States.

During the interview, the officer may ask you about any trips you have taken outside the United States and how long they lasted. One requirement for U.S. citizenship is that you must have *continuous residence* in the United States. In general, to have *continuous residence* you must not leave the United States for more than six months.

2 | WATCH

A V1 S5 Watch the video. Did Mrs. Rivas take any trips outside of the United States for more than six months?

B V1 S5 Watch the video again. Complete the sentences. Circle *a*, *b*, or *c*.

1. Mrs. Rivas left the country _____.
   a. three or four times
   b. five or six times
   c. six or seven times

2. She said she traveled to _____.
   a. Texas
   b. Mexico
   c. Guatemala

3. Mrs. Rivas traveled in 2000 because her sister _____.
   a. got married
   b. was sick
   c. had a baby

4. She traveled in 2006 because her _____.
   a. sister got married
   b. son was born
   c. husband's mother was sick

3 SPEAKING STRATEGY   Stalling for time

Sometimes you may need time to think about your answer to a question. To stall for time, you can say *Let me think* or *One minute, please.* You can also say *Uhm* or *Uh.* Another way to give yourself more time is to repeat the question. This way the officer knows you understand the question and are thinking about your answer.

A T072 🔊 Listen to part of Mrs. Rivas's naturalization interview. What does she say to stall for time? Write the **two** expressions she uses.

1. _____   2. _____

B Here are ways to stall for time.

One minute, please.   Let me think.

Give me a minute, please.   Let me think about that for a minute.

4 PRONUNCIATION

Pronunciation Watch

Final consonant sounds

It is important to pronounce the final consonant sound in a word. If the final sound includes more than one consonant, then the two consonants are pronounced quickly and together.

T073 🔊 **Listen and repeat.**

Have you traveled much outside the United States?

Did any of those trips last more than six months?

We went to Mexico when my husband's mother was sick.

Show what you know!

ROLE-PLAY. PAIRS. Look at your own N-400 Application. Give Part 7 to your partner. Student A, you are the officer. Ask questions about the applicant's trips outside the United States.
Student B, you are the applicant. Stall for time as you answer the questions.

Can you… stall for time? ☐

Lesson 5 Using clear pronunciation and self-correcting

1 BEFORE YOU WATCH

A Go to pages 183 and 184. Look at Part 8 of the N-400 Application and the glossed words. This section asks about your marital history.

B The officer may ask you about details of your marital status. What are some possible questions?

_____

_____

_____

_____

2 WATCH

A V1 S6 Watch the video. How many times has Mrs. Rivas been married?

B V1 S6 Watch the video again. Write *T* for True or *F* for False.

_____ 1. The officer asks Mrs. Rivas for her marriage certificate.

_____ 2. Mrs. Rivas's husband is from Mexico.

_____ 3. Mrs. Rivas is a widow.

_____ 4. Mrs. Rivas's husband has been married before.

_____ 5. Mrs. Rivas was not married before.

3 SPEAKING STRATEGY | Using clear pronunciation and self-correcting

During the interview, you may mispronounce words or you may choose a wrong word or expression when you speak. It is okay to repeat the words you mispronounce more clearly so that the officer can understand you. If you use the wrong word, you can self-correct and then repeat your answer. No one expects you to speak perfect English!

A T074 🔊 **Listen to part of Mrs. Rivas's naturalization interview. Mrs. Rivas makes a mistake pronouncing a word and then self-corrects. What word is she trying to say?**

B **Here are ways to practice pronunciation.**

- Use the Record and Compare interactive practice activity on your Active Book DVD-ROM.
- Review each section of the N-400 application. Practice saying the words in each section.
- Practice your interview with a native speaker. Ask him or her to correct your pronunciation.

4 PRONUNCIATION

Pronunciation Watch

Falling Intonation with Statements
When we make statements in English, our voice goes down at the end. This is called falling intonation.

T075
🔊 **Listen and repeat.**

He is Mexican.

He is taking his test today.

I was never married before.

Show what you know!

ROLE-PLAY. PAIRS. Look at your own N-400 Application. Give Part 8 to your partner. Student A, you are the officer. Ask questions about the applicant's marital status. Student B, you are the applicant. Use clear pronunciation and self-correct any mistakes.

Can you... use clear pronunciation and self-correct? ☐

1 BEFORE YOU WATCH

A Go to page 185. Look at Part 9 of the N-400 Application and the glossed words. This section asks for information about your children.

B The officer may ask you questions about how many children you have, if they are U.S. citizens, and where they live. What are some possible questions?

_____

_____

_____

2 WATCH

A V1 S7 Watch the video. Did Mrs. Rivas list all of her children on her N-400 application?

B V1 S7 Watch the video again. Answer the questions. Circle a, b, or c.

1. How many daughters does Mrs. Rivas have?
   a. one
   b. two
   c. three

2. How many children does she have?
   a. two
   b. three
   c. four

3. How old is Mrs. Rivas's oldest child?
   a. twenty
   b. twenty-one
   c. twenty-two

4. Where were her children born?
   a. Mexico
   b. California
   c. Texas

3 SPEAKING STRATEGY — Responding to requests for clarification

During the interview, the officer may not understand your answers. The officer may repeat the same question or say it in a different way. You can repeat the question to make sure you understand it. If necessary, use different words to try to make your answer clearer. Speak calmly and slowly.

A T076 🔊 **Listen to part of Mrs. Rivas's naturalization interview. What does she say when the officer requests clarification?**

a. I have another son, Arturo Junior, but he is not a child. He is twenty years old.

b. I have another son, Arturo. But he is twenty years old.

B Here are examples of ways to respond to requests for clarification.

Are you asking me if I have another son? Yes, I do.

I'm sorry, maybe I was not clear. Yes, I have another son.

Let me explain. Yes, I do have another son, but he doesn't live at home anymore.

4 PRONUNCIATION

Pronunciation Watch

Th sounds

In English, there are two *th* sounds. The sound of *th* in *this* and *they* is a voiced sound. The sound of *th* in *three* and *oath* is a voiceless sound. To make the *th* sound, put your tongue between your teeth. Look at the diagram to help you.

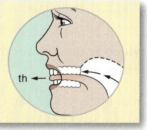

th ←

T077 🔊 **Listen and repeat.**

Thank you.

We went in 2006. (two **th**ousand six)

I have **th**ree children.

That's why he is here.

They were born in California.

Do you have ano**th**er child?

Show what you know!

ROLE-PLAY. PAIRS. Look at your own N-400 Application. Give Part 9 to your partner. Student A, you are the officer. Ask questions about the applicant's children. Ask your partner to clarify his or her answers.
Student B, you are the applicant. Respond to your partner's request for clarification.

Can you... respond to requests for clarification? ☐

LESSON 1 USING POLITE EXPRESSIONS

1 BEFORE YOU WATCH

A Go to page 185. Look at Part 10A of the N-400 Application and the glossed words. This section asks general information about you.

B The officer may ask you about voting, claiming to be a U.S. citizen, or paying taxes. What are some possible questions?

_____

_____

_____

2 WATCH

A **V2 S3** Watch the video. Does Mr. Gao pay his taxes?

B **V2 S3** Watch the video again. Answer the questions. Circle *a* or *b*.

1. Which statement is true about Mr. Gao?
   a. He wrote on a form that he is an American citizen.
   b. He did not tell anyone that he is an American citizen.

2. Why does the officer ask Mr. Gao if he has voted in U.S. elections?
   a. She wants to make sure he knows that he cannot vote yet.
   b. She wants to tell him about his voting rights in Florida.

3. What does fail to file your taxes mean?
   a. You fill out the forms to pay your taxes.
   b. You don't fill out the forms to pay your taxes.

4. What does Mr. Gao say that good businessmen do?
   a. They pay their taxes to the government.
   b. They pay all of their bills on time.

During the interview, you may need to ask the officer to repeat or to clarify something or you may need to check your understanding. You can use a polite expression to begin, such as *Excuse me* or *I'm sorry.*

A   T078   🔊   Listen to part of Mr. Gao's naturalization interview. Mr. Gao checks his understanding. What polite expression does he use?

B   Here are ways to begin a question when you need to clarify, check your understanding, or ask for repetition.

Excuse me . . .

Pardon me . . .

Sorry. . .

I'm sorry. . .

4   PRONUNCIATION

Pronunciation Watch

Unstressed sounds in *a*, *an*, and *the*

The words *a*, *an,* and *the* are not stressed in English. This means the vowel sound is very short and quiet. Other words in the sentence will be stressed.

T079
🔊   Listen and repeat.

Let me ask you **a** few general questions.

I worked as **a** chef.

I am not **an** American citizen.

Did you file **an** income tax return?

Are you still at **the** same address?

I pay taxes to **the** government.

Show what you know!

ROLE-PLAY. PAIRS. Look at your own N-400 Application. Give Part 10A to your partner. Student A, you are the officer. Ask the applicant the general questions using polite expressions. Student B, you are the applicant. Answer the questions politely.

Can you. . . use polite expressions? ☐

LESSON 2 ASKING FOR DEFINITIONS OR EXPLANATIONS

1   BEFORE YOU WATCH

A Go to page 186. Look at Parts 10B and 10C of the N-400 Application and the glossed words. This section asks about affiliations and continuous residence.

B The officer may ask you about organizations or associations you may have joined. The officer may also ask if you have ever identified yourself as a non-resident. What are some possible questions?

_____

_____

_____

2   WATCH

A **V2 S4** ▶️ Watch the video. Has Mr. Gao ever belonged to any associations or organizations?

B **V2 S4** ▶️ Watch the video again. Complete the sentences. Circle *a* or *b*.

1. Mr. Gao has been a member of _____.
   a. some hotel associations
   b. some restaurant associations

2. The officer asks Mr. Gao if he ever belonged to _____.
   a. the Nazi Party
   b. the Communist Party

3. The officer asks Mr. Gao if he ever tried to _____ a government.
   a. overthrow
   b. overturn

SPEAKING STRATEGY Asking for a definition or explanation

> During the interview, you may not understand some words or expressions the officer uses. Sometimes it helps to have a definition or explanation of the word. To ask for a definition or explanation, you can say *Can you tell me what that means?* or *Can you explain what _____ means?*

T080

A 🔊 **Listen to part of Mr. Gao's naturalization interview. What does he ask the officer? Circle *a* or *b*.**

a. I'm sorry. Could you please explain what *overthrow* means?

b. Sorry. I don't understand what *overthrow* means. Can you explain?

B **Here are ways to ask someone to explain or define a word.**

I'm sorry. Can you explain _____.   Excuse me, what does _____ mean?

Could you please explain _____.   I'm sorry. I don't know what that means.

Can you tell me what _____ means?

4

PRONUNCIATION

Pronunciation Watch

Linking consonants and vowels

When we speak, we often link words in a phrase together. Consonant sounds at the end of one word are linked to the next word if it begins with a vowel sound. The consonant and vowel sounds are linked together, so the two words almost sound like one word.

T081

🔊 **Listen and repeat.**

I'm a member of a restaurant association.

Have you ever been a member of the Communist Party?

Have you ever advocated the overthrow of any government?

Show what you know!

ROLE-PLAY. PAIRS. Look at your own N-400 Application. Give Parts 10B and 10C to your partner. Student A, you are the officer. Ask questions about the applicant's affiliations and continuous residence. Student B, you are the applicant. Practice asking your partner for definitions and explanations.

Can you...ask for a definition or an explanation? ☐

LESSON 3 SELF-CORRECTING YOUR GRAMMAR

1 BEFORE YOU WATCH

A Go to page 187. Look at Part 10D of the N-400 Application and the glossed words. This section asks about your moral character.

B The officer may ask you about being stopped by the police, giving false information, and other questions about how you behave in public. What are some possible questions?

_____

_____

_____

2 WATCH

A **V2 S5** ◀ Watch the video. The officer asks Mr. Gao about his experience with the police or military. Has Mr. Gao ever served in the military?

B **V2 S5** ◀ Watch the video again. The officer asks questions with *Have you ever . . .?* Check (✓) what the officer asks about.

☐ **1.** committed a crime or offense for which you were not arrested

☐ **2.** stolen anything

☐ **3.** been arrested

☐ **4.** been cited

☐ **5.** been detained

☐ **6.** received a speeding ticket

3 SPEAKING STRATEGY   Self-correcting your grammar

> During the interview, you may make grammar mistakes as you answer the officer's questions. You can stop and correct yourself. You can say, *I meant to say* or *What I mean is*.

A T082 🔊)) **Listen to part of Mr. Gao's naturalization interview. Mr. Gao corrects a grammar mistake. What is he trying to say?**

B **Here are ways to self-correct.**

I mean . . .   I meant to say . . .   That's not what I mean. What I mean is . . .

4 PRONUNCIATION

Pronunciation Watch

Final sounds + -ed
Verbs with final sounds of *t* and *d* add an extra syllable /Id/. For verbs that end with other final sounds, the *–ed* is pronounced /d/ or /t/ and does not add an extra syllable.

A T083 🔊)) **Listen and repeat.**

/Id/	/d/	/t/
arrested	detained	finished
convicted	received	placed
cited	entered	stopped

B T084 🔊)) **Listen and repeat.**

Have you ever been arrested?

I've never been detained.

Have you ever committed a crime?

Show what you know!

ROLE-PLAY. PAIRS. Look at your own N-400 Application. Give Part 10D to your partner. Student A, you are the officer. Ask questions about the applicant's moral character. Student B, you are the applicant. As you speak, self-correct any grammar mistakes you make.

Can you. . . self-correct your grammar mistakes? ☐

LESSON 4 RESPONDING APPROPRIATELY TO QUESTIONS

1 BEFORE YOU WATCH

A Go to page 188. Look at Parts 10E, 10F, and 10G of the N-400 Application and the glossed words. This section asks about deportation, military service, and selective service registration.

B The officer may ask you about any deportation or legal orders against you. The officer may also ask if you have ever served in the armed forces or, if you are a man, if you have registered for the Selective Service. What are some possible questions?

_____

_____

_____

_____

2 WATCH

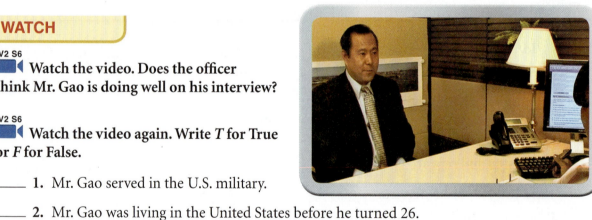

A V2 S6 🎬 Watch the video. Does the officer think Mr. Gao is doing well on his interview?

B V2 S6 🎬 Watch the video again. Write *T* for True or *F* for False.

_____ **1.** Mr. Gao served in the U.S. military.

_____ **2.** Mr. Gao was living in the United States before he turned 26.

_____ **3.** Mr. Gao came to the United States when he was 22.

_____ **4.** Mr. Gao registered for the Selective Service.

3 SPEAKING STRATEGY Responding appropriately to questions

During the interview, the officer will ask you many questions that only require a *yes* or *no* response. For example, *Have you ever been deported? Have you served in the U.S. Armed Forces?* In general, you should give concise, or short, answers. Do not add any unnecessary information.

A T085 🔊 Listen to part of Mr. Gao's naturalization interview. Describe how he answers the officer's questions.

B Here are ways to answer questions appropriately.

- Always use polite, formal language. You are speaking with a government official.
- Keep your answers short, but make sure to include all the information the officer needs.
- Make sure to ask for clarification or repetition if you did not understand or hear a question.
- Try not to interrupt the officer unless it is absolutely necessary.

4 PRONUNCIATION

Pronunciation Watch

Compound nouns

Compound nouns are nouns that are made up of two nouns, for example, *naturalization interview* and *English test*. In compound nouns, the first word is stressed.

T086 🔊 **Listen and repeat.**

- armed forces
- tax return
- Selective Service
- United States

Show what you know!

ROLE-PLAY. PAIRS. Look at your own N-400 Application. Give Parts 10E, 10F, and 10G to your partner. Student A, you are the officer. Ask the applicant questions about military service and the Selective Service.
Student B, you are the applicant. Practice giving short and clear answers.

Can you... respond appropriately to questions? ☐

LESSON 5 ASKING FOR AN EXAMPLE

1 BEFORE YOU WATCH

A Go to page 188. Look at Part 10H of the N-400 Application and the glossed words. This section asks about oath requirements.

B The officer will verify that you are willing to take the Oath of Allegiance. The officer wants to know if you understand what taking the oath means. What are some possible questions?

_____

_____

_____

_____

2 WATCH

A V2 S7  Watch the video. How has Mr. Gao been practicing the Oath of Allegiance?

B V2 S7 Watch the video again. Write *T* for True or *F* for False.

_____ 1. Mr. Gao knows that he will have to take the Oath of Allegiance.

_____ 2. Mr. Gao supports the Constitution of the United States.

_____ 3. Mr. Gao doesn't understand the Oath of Allegiance.

_____ 4. Mr. Gao is willing to take the Oath of Allegiance.

_____ 5. Mr. Gao isn't willing to perform noncombatant services if the law requires it.

3 SPEAKING STRATEGY   Asking for an example

During the interview, if you do not understand the officer, you can ask for an example. An example can help you check if you have understood the officer's question. You can say *Could you please give me an example?* You can also give an example so the officer can clarify the question in case you have not understood it.

A T087 🔊) **Listen to part of Mr. Gao's naturalization interview. How does he ask for an example? Circle *a* or *b*.**

a. Perform noncombatant services? Can I have an example?

b. Perform noncombatant services? Could you give an example?

B. **Here are different ways you can ask for an example.**

Could you give an example, please?

I don't understand. Can you give me an example?

Could I have an example?

4 PRONUNCIATION

Pronunciation Watch

Word stress: Words with three or more syllables

In English, the stressed syllable is longer and louder than the other syllables.

T088
🔊) **Listen and repeat.**

●
government

●
al**le**giance

●
national

●
u**ni**ted

●
services

●
im**por**tance

Show what you know!

ROLE-PLAY. PAIRS. Look at your own N-400 Application. Give Part 10H to your partner. Student A, you are the officer. Ask the applicant questions about taking the Oath of Allegiance. Student B, you are the applicant. Practice asking for examples.

Can you...ask for an example? ☐

LESSON 6 TAKING THE OATH OF ALLEGIANCE

1 READ

Go to page 172. Read the Oath of Allegiance. Study the glossed words and definitions.

2 WATCH

V2 S8

◀ Watch Mr. Gao practicing the Oath of Allegiance.

3 CHECK YOUR UNDERSTANDING

Read parts of the Oath of Allegiance. Choose the sentence with the closest meaning. Circle *a* or *b*.

1. *I hereby declare, on oath, that I absolutely and entirely renounce and abjure all allegiance and fidelity to any foreign prince, potentate, state, or sovereignty, of whom or which I have heretofore been a subject or citizen;*
   a. I won't be loyal to any other country or person anymore, only to the United States now.
   b. I won't be loyal to the United States and countries that are its friends.

2. *. . . that I will support and defend the Constitution and laws of the United States of America against all enemies, foreign and domestic. . .*
   a. I will support the Constitution and fight for the United States against enemies who are in America and around the world.
   b. I will read the Constitution and join the military of the United States to fight other countries around the world.

3. *. . .that I will bear true faith and allegiance to the same . . .*
   a. I will follow the Constitution and laws of the United States.
   b. I will follow the President and the people of the United States.

4. *. . . that I will bear arms on behalf of the United States when required by the law;*

    a. If the U.S. government asks me to fight with the military, I can say no.

    b. If the U.S. government asks me to fight with the military, I must say yes.

5. *. . . that I will perform noncombatant service in the armed forces of the United States when required by the law;*

    a. If the military asks me to help with jobs that don't include fighting, I can say no.

    b. If the military asks me to help with jobs that don't include fighting, I must say yes.

6. *. . . that I take this obligation freely, without any mental reservation or purpose of evasion, so help me God.*

    a. I am making these promises in the oath because someone has asked me to.

    b. I am making these promises in the oath because I really want to do this.

4 PRONUNCIATION

Pronunciation Watch

Thought groups

We use pauses to break sentences into smaller thought groups. These pauses organize the meaning of a sentence. This helps the listener understand. Punctuation marks, such as periods (.), commas (,), and semi-colons (;), show us places to pause.

A T089 🔊 **Go to page 172. Listen to the Oath of Allegiance. Mark (/) the thought groups.**

Example:

I hereby declare, / on oath, / that I absolutely and entirely renounce and abjure / . . .

B T089 🔊 **Listen again. Then practice the Oath of Allegiance.**

Show what you know!

DISCUSS. What does becoming a citizen of the United States mean to you? Explain your ideas.

Can you. . . say the Oath of Allegiance? ☐

The Oath of Allegiance

I hereby declare, on oath,[1] that I absolutely and entirely renounce and abjure[2] all allegiance and fidelity[3] to any foreign prince, potentate,[4] state, or sovereignty,[5] of whom or which I have heretofore[6] been a subject[7] or citizen; that I will support[8] and defend[9] the Constitution and laws of the United States of America against all enemies,[10] foreign[11] and domestic;[12] that I will bear true faith and allegiance to[13] the same; that I will bear arms on behalf of[14] the United States when required[15] by the law; that I will perform noncombatant service[16] in the armed forces[17] of the United States when required by the law; and that I take this obligation freely[18] without any mental reservation[19] or purpose of evasion[20]; so help me God.

[1] **hereby declare on oath** with this document, I promise
[2] **renounce and abjure** say in public that you give up something
[3] **allegiance and fidelity** loyalty (to a state)
[4] **potentate** someone who has the power to rule over others
[5] **sovereignty** supreme authority, or politically independent state
[6] **heretofore** before now
[7] **subject** a person under the rule of a king, queen, or other authority
[8] **support** to say in public and officially something that is true
[9] **defend** to protect something or someone
[10] **enemies** people who want to hurt or harm you
[11] **foreign** overseas (outside of the U.S.)
[12] **domestic** within the country (inside the U.S.)
[13] **bear true faith and allegiance to** to be faithful to
[14] **bear arms on behalf of** to use weapons to fight for someone
[15] **required** necessary
[16] **perform noncombatant service** to do work that does not require fighting with weapons
[17] **armed forces** U.S. Army, Air Force, Navy, Marines, Coast Guard
[18] **take this obligation freely** to promise by my own choice, without being forced by others
[19] **without any mental reservation** without any doubts
[20] **purpose of evasion** to avoid

PART ③ READING AND WRITING TEST PREP

OVERVIEW

During your interview, the officer will assess your ability to read and write in English. To pass the reading test, you must read a sentence aloud in a way that shows you understand its meaning.

To pass the writing test, you will listen to a sentence and must write clearly so that the officer can read the sentence.

To see the scoring guidelines for the Reading and Writing tests, go to the official USCIS website at www.uscis.gov or click on the Resources tab at the bottom of each Active Book screen.

FUTURE U.S. CITIZENS: THE STUDENT BOOK

Part 3 Reading and Writing Test Prep contains 64 practice sentences for you to read aloud and 64 practice sentences for you to write as dictation exercises. Both the reading and writing sentences will be about U.S. history and civics. To prepare for the reading and writing test, study the 100 Civics questions and answers. You can also study the USCIS reading and writing lists. Go to www.uscis.gov or click on the Resources tab at the bottom of each Active Book screen.

FUTURE U.S. CITIZENS: THE ACTIVE BOOK

Use the *Future U.S. Citizens* Active Book to help you study.

- The entire book is in digital form on the Active Book, so you can read and listen to the practice sentences on a computer. When you see ◄))), click on it to play the practice sentences.

- The Active Book contains extra record-and-compare reading practice activities. Use the exercises to listen to a model sentence, to record yourself reading the sentence aloud, and then to play your recording back to compare.

- The Active Book contains extra writing dictation exercises. Use the exercises to practice listening to a recorded sentence and then typing the words. Then click on Show Answers to see the sentence correctly typed and compare your answers.

Read the sentences aloud. Then play the audio. Listen and check your pronunciation.

T090   **1.** Why did the colonists come to America?

T091   **2.** Who lived in America before the colonists?

T092   **3.** Why were the colonists angry with Great Britain?

T093   **4.** What were two of the original states?

T094   **5.** When was the Declaration of Independence written?

T095   **6.** What did the Declaration of Independence give the colonists?

T096   **7.** Who was one of the writers of the Federalist Papers?

T097   **8.** Who wrote the Constitution?

T098   **9.** Who was George Washington?

T099 **10.** Why is Benjamin Franklin famous?

T100 **11.** Who did America fight during the War of 1812?

T101 **12.** What was the Louisiana Territory?

T102 **13.** What war ended slavery?

T103 **14.** What states wanted to keep slaves?

T104 **15.** Who was Abraham Lincoln?

T105 **16.** What document said slaves were free?

T106 **17.** What rights did Susan B. Anthony fight for?

T107 **18.** What does the Nineteenth Amendment do?

T108 **19.** Who was Woodrow Wilson?

T109 **20.** When did the United States enter World War II?

T110 **21.** What was the United States worried about during the Cold War?

T111 **22.** What is capitalism?

T112 **23.** Who was one leader of the civil rights movement?

T113 **24.** What was one goal of the civil rights movement?

T114 **25.** What happened to the World Trade Center in New York City?

T115 **26.** Why is September 11 an important day in American history?

T116 **27.** What protects the basic rights of Americans?

T117 **28.** When was the Constitution written?

T118 **29.** What is the Bill of Rights?

T119 **30.** What is protected in the First Amendment?

T120 **31.** What is Congress?

T121 **32.** Where is the Capitol building?

T122 33. What does the system of checks and balances do?

T123 34. What branch can declare a law unconstitutional?

T124 35. Who is the leader of the U.S. military?

T125 36. How many terms can the President serve?

T126 37. Who is the president of the Senate?

T127 38. What is the job of the Speaker of the House?

T128 39. Who advises the President?

T129 40. Who selects the members of the Cabinet?

T130 41. How many senators does each state have?

T131 42. Who does a senator represent?

T132 43. How many members of the House of Representatives does each state have?

T133 44. How many times can a member of the House of Representatives be elected?

T134 45. How are members of the Supreme Court selected?

T135 46. How long can a member of the Supreme Court serve?

T136 47. What are two powers of the federal government?

T137 48. What are two services a state government provides?

T138 49. Who is the head of the executive branch of state government?

T139 50. Where does the governor of a state live?

T140 51. What is one of the major political parties in the United States?

T141 52. What are primary elections?

T142 53. Which amendment gave women the right to vote?

T143 54. How old must a citizen be to vote in elections?

T144 55. What does the Selective Service require men to do?

T145 56. Why are citizens called to serve on a jury?

T146 57. What country is on the northern border of the United States?

T147 58. Where is the Atlantic Ocean?

T148 59. What is the Statue of Liberty?

T149 60. Who gave the Statue of Liberty to the United States?

T150 61. How many stripes are on the American flag?

T151 62. How many stars are on the American flag?

T152 63. When do we celebrate Martin Luther King, Jr.'s birthday?

T153 64. When do we celebrate Columbus Day?

Play the audio. Listen and write the sentence. Then check the answer key on pages 178–179.

T154   1. _____

T155   2. _____

T156   3. _____

T157   4. _____

T158   5. _____

T159   6. _____

T160   7. _____

T161   8. _____

T162   9. _____

T163   10. _____

T164   11. _____

T165   12. _____

T166   13. _____

T167   14. _____

T168   15. _____

T169   16. _____

T170   17. _____

T171   18. _____

T172   19. _____

T173   20. _____

T174   21. _____

T175   22. _____

T176   23. _____

T177   24. _____

T178   25. _____

T179   26. _____

T180   27. _____

T181   28. _____

T182   29. _____

T183   30. _____

T184   31. _____

T185   32. _____

T186 33. _____

T187 34. _____

T188 35. _____

T189 36. _____

T190 37. _____

T191 38. _____

T192 39. _____

T193 40. _____

T194 41. _____

T195 42. _____

T196 43. _____

T197 44. _____

T198 45. _____

T199 46. _____

T200 47. _____

T201 48. _____

T202 49. _____

T203 50. _____

T204 51. _____

T205 52. _____

T206 53. _____

T207 54. _____

T208 55. _____

T209 56. _____

T210 57. _____

T211 58. _____

T212 59. _____

T213 60. _____

T214 61. _____

T215 62. _____

T216 63. _____

T217 64. _____

1. The colonists came to America because they wanted religious freedom.

2. Native Americans lived in America before the colonists.

3. The colonists were angry with Great Britain because of high taxes.

4. Two of the original states were New York and Maryland.

5. The Declaration of Independence was written in 1776.

6. The Declaration of Independence gave colonists freedom from Great Britain.

7. John Jay was one of the writers of the Federalist Papers.

8. The Founding Fathers wrote the Constitution.

9. George Washington was the first President.

10. Benjamin Franklin is famous because he started the first free libraries.

11. America fought the British in the War of 1812.

12. America bought land called the Louisiana Territory from France.

13. The Civil War ended slavery.

14. The southern states wanted to keep slaves.

15. Abraham Lincoln was the sixteenth president of the United States.

16. The Emancipation Proclamation said slaves were free.

17. Susan B. Anthony fought for civil rights.

18. The Nineteenth Amendment gives women the right to vote.

19. Woodrow Wilson was President during World War I.

20. The United States entered World War II in 1941.

21. The United States was worried about communism during the Cold War.

22. Capitalism is the economic system in the United States.

23. Martin Luther King, Jr. was a leader of the civil rights movement.

24. The civil rights movement wanted equal rights for everyone.

25. The World Trade Center in New York City was attacked by terrorists.

26. September 11, 2001 is important because the United States was attacked by terrorists.

27. The Constitution protects the basic rights of Americans.

28. The Constitution was written in 1787.

29. The Bill of Rights includes the first ten amendments to the Constitution.

30. The freedom of speech and religion are protected in the First Amendment.

31. Congress is the legislative branch of the government.

32. The Capitol building is in Washington, D.C.

33. Checks and balances stop a government branch from becoming too powerful.

34. The judicial branch can declare a law unconstitutional.

35. The President is the Commander in Chief of the U.S. military.

36. The President can only serve two terms.

37. The Vice President is the president of the Senate.

38. The Speaker of the House presides over the House of Representatives.

39. The Cabinet advises the President.

40. The President selects the members of the Cabinet.

41. Each state has two senators.

42. A senator represents all of the people in the state.

43. The total population of a state determines the number of members in the House of Representatives.

44. Members of the House of Representatives can be elected as many times as they run for office.

45. The members of the Supreme Court are selected by the President.

46. A Supreme Court member can serve for life.

47. The federal government can create an army and declare war.

48. A state government provides schooling and a driver's license.

49. The governor is the head of the executive branch of state government.

50. The governor of a state lives in the capital city of the state.

51. One of the major political parties is the Republican party.

52. Primary elections help inform the public about the party candidates.

53. The Nineteenth Amendment gave women the right to vote.

54. A citizen must be eighteen years old to vote in elections.

55. The Selective Service requires all men between 18 and 25 to register for military service.

56. It is a civic responsibility to serve on a jury.

57. Canada is on the northern border of the United States.

58. The Atlantic Ocean is to the east of the United States.

59. The Statue of Liberty is a symbol of freedom.

60. France gave the Statue of Liberty to the United States.

61. There are thirteen stripes on the American flag.

62. There are fifty stars on the American flag.

63. We celebrate Martin Luther King, Jr.'s birthday in January.

64. We celebrate Columbus Day in October.

OMB No. 1615-0052; Expires 01/31/11

Department of Homeland Security
U.S Citizenship and Immigration Services

**N-400 Application
for Naturalization**

Print clearly or type your answers using CAPITAL letters. Failure to print clearly may delay your application. Use black ink.

Part 1. Your Name *(Person applying for naturalization)*

A. Your current legal name.

Family Name *(Last Name)*

Given Name *(First Name)*

Full Middle Name *(If applicable)*

B. Your name **exactly** as it appears on your Permanent Resident Card.

Family Name *(Last Name)*

Given Name *(First Name)*

Full Middle Name *(If applicable)*

C. If you have ever used other names, provide them below.

Family Name *(Last Name)*	Given Name *(First Name)*	Middle Name

D. Name change *(optional)*

Read the Instructions before you decide whether to change your name.

1. Would you like to legally change your name? ☐ Yes ☐ No

2. If "Yes," print the new name you would like to use. Do not use initials or abbreviations when writing your new name.

Family Name *(Last Name)*

Given Name *(First Name)*

Full Middle Name

Part 2. Information About Your Eligibility *(Check only one)*

I am at least 18 years old **AND**

A. ☐ I have been a lawful permanent resident of the United States for at least five years.

B. ☐ I have been a lawful permanent resident of the United States for at least three years, **and** I have been married to and living with the same U.S. citizen for the last three years, **and** my spouse has been a U.S. citizen for the last three years.

C. ☐ I am applying on the basis of qualifying military service.

D. ☐ Other *(Explain)* _____

Write your USCIS A-Number here:
A

For USCIS Use Only

Bar Code	Date Stamp
	Remarks

Action Block

Form N-400 (Rev. 04/05/10) Y

---

failure when you do not do something properly

delay make something (your application) happen more slowly

current what is true now

if applicable if it affects you

exactly the same way

legally allowed by law

initial(s) the first letter(s) of a name

abbreviations the short form of a name; for example, do not write Wm. or Will if you would like to have the name William.

eligibility the right to apply for something

lawful permanent resident a person who is living legally in the United States; also known as a permanent resident alien, a resident alien permit holder, or a green card holder

spouse your husband or wife

Part 3. Information About You

Write your USCIS A-Number here:
A

A. U.S. Social Security Number   **B.** Date of Birth *(mm/dd/yyyy)*   **C.** Date You Became a Permanent Resident *(mm/dd/yyyy)*

D. Country of Birth   **E.** Country of Nationality

F. Are either of your parents U.S. citizens? *(If yes, see instructions)*   ☐ Yes   ☐ No

G. What is your current marital status?   ☐ Single, Never Married   ☐ Married   ☐ Divorced   ☐ Widowed

☐ Marriage Annulled or Other *(Explain)* _____

H. Are you requesting a waiver of the English and/or U.S. History and Government requirements based on a disability or impairment and attaching Form N-648 with your application?   ☐ Yes   ☐ No

I. Are you requesting an accommodation to the naturalization process because of a disability or impairment? *(See instructions for some examples of accommodations.)*   ☐ Yes   ☐ No

If you answered "Yes," check the box below that applies:

☐ I am deaf or hearing impaired and need a sign language interpreter who uses the following language: _____

☐ I use a wheelchair.

☐ I am blind or sight impaired.

☐ I will need another type of accommodation. Explain: _____

_____

_____

Part 4. Addresses and Telephone Numbers

A. Home Address - Street Number and Name *(Do not write a P.O. Box in this space.)*   Apartment Number

City   County   State   ZIP Code   Country

B. Care of   Mailing Address - Street Number and Name *(If different from home address)*   Apartment Number

City   State   ZIP Code   Country

C. Daytime Phone Number *(If any)*   Evening Phone Number *(If any)*   E-Mail Address *(If any)*
(   )   (   )

Form N-400 (Rev. 04/05/10) Y Page 2

---

marital status if you are single, married, divorced, or widowed

widowed your marital status if your husband or wife has died

annulled something officially and legally ended as if it had never happened

waiver an official written statement saying you don't have to do something

disability a physical or mental condition that makes it difficult for you to do things

impairment a physical or mental condition that limits your abilities

accommodation a change in the way something is done for you

deaf unable to hear

hearing impaired unable to hear well

sign language interpreter a person who uses hand signs to translate for applicants who are deaf or hearing impaired

blind unable to see

Part 5. Information for Criminal Records Search

Write your USCIS A-Number here:
A

NOTE: The categories below are those required by the FBI. See instructions for more information.

A. Gender

☐ Male ☐ Female

B. Height

| Feet | Inches |

C. Weight

| Pounds |

D. Are you Hispanic or Latino? ☐ Yes ☐ No

E. Race (Select one or more)

☐ White ☐ Asian ☐ Black or African American ☐ American Indian or Alaskan Native ☐ Native Hawaiian or Other Pacific Islander

F. Hair color

☐ Black ☐ Brown ☐ Blonde ☐ Gray ☐ White ☐ Red ☐ Sandy ☐ Bald (No Hair)

G. Eye color

☐ Brown ☐ Blue ☐ Green ☐ Hazel ☐ Gray ☐ Black ☐ Pink ☐ Maroon ☐ Other

Part 6. Information About Your Residence and Employment

A. Where have you lived during the last five years? Begin with where you live now and then list every place you lived for the last five years. If you need more space, use a separate sheet of paper.

Street Number and Name, Apartment Number, City, State, Zip Code, and Country	Dates (mm/dd/yyyy)	
	From	To
Current Home Address - Same as Part 4.A		Present

B. Where have you worked (or, if you were a student, what schools did you attend) during the last five years? Include military service. Begin with your current or latest employer and then list every place you have worked or studied for the last five years. If you need more space, use a separate sheet of paper.

Employer or School Name	Employer or School Address (Street, City, and State)	Dates (mm/dd/yyyy)		Your Occupation
		From	To	

Form N-400 (Rev. 04/05/10) Y Page 3

gender male or female

height how tall you are

weight how much you weigh (Note: *pounds* are used in the United States for weight)

residence where you live; your home

employment your job history

employer person, company, or organization that you work for

occupation your job or profession

Part 7. Time Outside the United States
(Including Trips to Canada, Mexico and the Caribbean Islands)

Write your USCIS A-Number here:
A

A. How many total days did you spend outside of the United States during the past five years? [ ] days

B. How many trips of 24 hours or more have you taken outside of the United States during the past five years? [ ] trips

C. List below all the trips of 24 hours or more that you have taken outside of the United States since becoming a lawful permanent resident. Begin with your most recent trip. If you need more space, use a separate sheet of paper.

Date You Left the United States (mm/dd/yyyy)	Date You Returned to the United States (mm/dd/yyyy)	Did Trip Last Six Months or More?	Countries to Which You Traveled	Total Days Out of the United States
		☐ Yes ☐ No		
		☐ Yes ☐ No		
		☐ Yes ☐ No		
		☐ Yes ☐ No		
		☐ Yes ☐ No		
		☐ Yes ☐ No		
		☐ Yes ☐ No		
		☐ Yes ☐ No		
		☐ Yes ☐ No		
		☐ Yes ☐ No		

Part 8. Information About Your Marital History

A. How many times have you been married (including annulled marriages)? [ ] If you have **never** been married, go to Part 9.

B. If you are now married, give the following information about your spouse:

1. Spouse's Family Name (*Last Name*)   Given Name (*First Name*)   Full Middle Name (*If applicable*)

2. Date of Birth (*mm/dd/yyyy*)   **3.** Date of Marriage (*mm/dd/yyyy*)   **4.** Spouse's U.S. Social Security #

5. Home Address - Street Number and Name   Apartment Number

City   State   Zip Code

annulled something officially and legally ended as if it had never happened
spouse your husband or wife

Part 8. Information About Your Marital History *(Continued)*

Write your USCIS A-Number here:
A

C. Is your spouse a U.S. citizen? ☐ Yes ☐ No

D. If your spouse is a U.S. citizen, give the following information:

    1. When did your spouse become a U.S. citizen? ☐ At Birth ☐ Other

    If "Other," give the following information:

    2. Date your spouse became a U.S. citizen

    3. Place your spouse became a U.S. citizen *(See instructions)*

    City and State

E. If your spouse is **not** a U.S. citizen, give the following information :

    1. Spouse's Country of Citizenship

    2. Spouse's USCIS A- Number *(If applicable)*
    A

    3. Spouse's Immigration Status
    ☐ Lawful Permanent Resident ☐ Other

F. If you were married before, provide the following information about your ==prior== spouse. If you have more than one ==previous== marriage, use a separate sheet of paper to provide the information requested in Questions 1-5 below.

    1. Prior Spouse's Family Name *(Last Name)* Given Name *(First Name)* Full Middle Name *(If applicable)*

    2. Prior Spouse's ==Immigration Status==
    ☐ U.S. Citizen
    ☐ Lawful Permanent Resident
    ☐ Other

    3. Date of Marriage *(mm/dd/yyyy)*

    4. Date Marriage Ended *(mm/dd/yyyy)*

    5. How Marriage Ended
    ☐ Divorce ☐ Spouse Died ☐ Other

G. How many times has your current spouse been married (including annulled marriages)? ☐

    If your spouse has **ever** been married before, give the following information about **your spouse's** prior marriage.
    If your spouse has more than one previous marriage, use a separate sheet(s) of paper to provide the information requested in Questions 1 - 5 below.

    1. Prior Spouse's Family Name *(Last Name)* Given Name *(First Name)* Full Middle Name *(If applicable)*

    2. Prior Spouse's Immigration Status
    ☐ U.S. Citizen
    ☐ Lawful Permanent Resident
    ☐ Other

    3. Date of Marriage *(mm/dd/yyyy)*

    4. Date Marriage Ended *(mm/dd/yyyy)*

    5. How Marriage Ended
    ☐ Divorce ☐ Spouse Died ☐ Other

Form N-400 (Rev. 04/05/10) Y Page 5

prior earlier

previous happening before now

immigration status a person's situation with the U.S. government

Part 9. Information About Your Children

Write your USCIS A-Number here:
A

A. How many sons and daughters have you had? For more information on which sons and daughters you should include and how to complete this section, see the Instructions.

B. Provide the following information about all of your sons and daughters. If you need more space, use a separate sheet of paper.

Full Name of Son or Daughter	Date of Birth (mm/dd/yyyy)	USCIS A- number (if child has one)	Country of Birth	Current Address (Street, City, State and Country)
		A		
		A		
		A		
		A		
		A		
		A		
		A		
		A		

[Add Children]   [Go to continuation page]

Part 10. Additional Questions

Answer Questions 1 through 14. If you answer "Yes" to any of these questions, include a written explanation with this form. Your written explanation should (1) explain why your answer was "Yes" and (2) provide any additional information that helps to explain your answer.

A. General Questions.

1. Have you **ever claimed** to be a U.S. citizen *(in writing or any other way)*? ☐ Yes ☐ No
2. Have you **ever registered** to vote in any Federal, State, or local election in the United States? ☐ Yes ☐ No
3. Have you **ever** voted in any Federal, State, or local election in the United States? ☐ Yes ☐ No
4. Since becoming a lawful permanent resident, have you **ever failed to file** a required Federal, State, or local tax return? ☐ Yes ☐ No
5. Do you owe any Federal, State, or local taxes that are **overdue**? ☐ Yes ☐ No
6. Do you have any **title of nobility** in any foreign country? ☐ Yes ☐ No
7. Have you ever been **declared legally incompetent** or been confined to a **mental institution** within the last five years? ☐ Yes ☐ No

Form N-400 (Rev. 04/05/10) Y Page 6

children sons and/or daughters

claim say something is true, even though it may not be true

register put your name on an official list

fail to file a tax return not submit your income tax forms to the government

overdue late in being done

title of nobility if you are a member of a noble or royal family in another country; for example, a prince or princess, a duke or duchess

be declared legally incompetent when the court says that you are unable to understand because of mental illness or mental impairment

mental institution a place where people with serious mental illnesses live and receive treatment

Part 10. Additional Questions *(Continued)*	Write your USCIS A-Number here: A

B. Affiliations.

8. a Have you **ever** been a member of or associated with any organization, association, fund foundation, party, club, society, or similar group in the United States or in any other place? ☐ Yes ☐ No

   b. If you answered "Yes," list the name of each group below. If you need more space, attach the names of the other group(s) on a separate sheet of paper.

Name of Group	Name of Group
1.	6.
2.	7.
3.	8.
4.	9.
5.	10.

9. Have you **ever** been a member of or in any way associated *(either directly or indirectly)* with:

   a. The Communist Party? ☐ Yes ☐ No

   b. Any other totalitarian party? ☐ Yes ☐ No

   c. A terrorist organization? ☐ Yes ☐ No

10. Have you **ever** advocated *(either directly or indirectly)* the overthrow of any government by force or violence? ☐ Yes ☐ No

11. Have you **ever** persecuted *(either directly or indirectly)* any person because of race, religion, national origin, membership in a particular social group, or political opinion? ☐ Yes ☐ No

12. Between March 23, 1933, and May 8, 1945, did you work for or associate in any way *(either directly or indirectly)* with:

   a. The Nazi government of Germany? ☐ Yes ☐ No

   b. Any government in any area (1) occupied by, (2) allied with, or (3) established with the help of the Nazi government of Germany? ☐ Yes ☐ No

   c. Any German, Nazi, or S.S. military unit, paramilitary unit, self-defense unit, vigilante unit, citizen unit, police unit, government agency or office, extermination camp, concentration camp, prisoner of war camp, prison, labor camp, or transit camp? ☐ Yes ☐ No

C. Continuous Residence.

Since becoming a lawful permanent resident of the United States:

13. Have you **ever** called yourself a "nonresident" on a Federal, State, or local tax return? ☐ Yes ☐ No

14. Have you **ever** failed to file a Federal, State, or local tax return because you considered yourself to be a "nonresident"? ☐ Yes ☐ No

Form N-400 (Rev. 04/05/10) Y Page 7

---

association an organization of people who do the same type of work or are similar in another way

totalitarian a political system in which the people have no power and are controlled by the government

terrorist a person or organization that uses violent actions against ordinary people or a government

advocate to publicly support a particular way of doing things

overthrow to remove a leader or government from power by using force

persecute to treat someone cruelly and unfairly because of his or her ideas

occupy to take over and control a place by military force

ally with to join with a group or government

since becoming from the time you became

nonresident someone who does not live permanently in the United States

Part 10. Additional Questions *(continued)*

Write your USCIS A-Number here:
A

D. Good Moral Character.

For the purposes of this application, you must answer "Yes" to the following questions, if applicable, even if your records were sealed or otherwise cleared or if anyone, including a judge, law enforcement officer, or attorney, told you that you no longer have a record.

15. Have you **ever** committed a crime or offense for which you were **not** arrested? ☐ Yes ☐ No

16. Have you **ever** been arrested, cited, or detained by any law enforcement officer (including USCIS or former INS and military officers) for any reason? ☐ Yes ☐ No

17. Have you **ever** been charged with committing any crime or offense? ☐ Yes ☐ No

18. Have you **ever** been convicted of a crime or offense? ☐ Yes ☐ No

19. Have you **ever** been placed in an alternative sentencing or a rehabilitative program (for example: diversion, deferred prosecution, withheld adjudication, deferred adjudication)? ☐ Yes ☐ No

20. Have you **ever** received a suspended sentence, been placed on probation, or been paroled? ☐ Yes ☐ No

21. Have you **ever** been in jail or prison? ☐ Yes ☐ No

If you answered "Yes" to any of Questions 15 through 21, complete the following table. If you need more space, use a separate sheet of paper to give the same information.

Why were you arrested, cited, detained, or charged?	Date arrested, cited, detained, or charged? *(mm/dd/yyyy)*	Where were you arrested, cited, detained, or charged? *(City, State, Country)*	Outcome or disposition of the arrest, citation, detention, or charge *(No charges filed, charges dismissed, jail, probation, etc.)*

Answer Questions 22 through 33. If you answer "Yes" to any of these questions, attach (1) your written explanation why your answer was "Yes" and (2) any additional information or documentation that helps explain your answer.

22. Have you **ever**:

   a. Been a habitual drunkard? ☐ Yes ☐ No

   b. Been a prostitute, or procured anyone for prostitution? ☐ Yes ☐ No

   c. Sold or smuggled controlled substances, illegal drugs, or narcotics? ☐ Yes ☐ No

   d. Been married to more than one person at the same time? ☐ Yes ☐ No

   e. Helped anyone enter or try to enter the United States illegally? ☐ Yes ☐ No

   f. Gambled illegally or received income from illegal gambling? ☐ Yes ☐ No

   g. Failed to support your dependents or to pay alimony? ☐ Yes ☐ No

23. Have you **ever** given false or misleading information to any U.S. Government official while applying for any immigration benefit or to prevent deportation, exclusion, or removal? ☐ Yes ☐ No

24. Have you **ever** lied to any U.S. Government official to gain entry or admission into the United States? ☐ Yes ☐ No

Form N-400 (Rev. 04/05/10) Y Page 8

good moral character behavior that is based on strong principles about what is right and wrong

commit a crime do something illegal

cite order to appear in court or pay a fine for doing something illegal

detain when the police stop and hold you for questioning

charge when the police give a formal statement that you have done something illegal

offense a crime

convict find someone guilty of a crime in a court of law

defer delay until a later date

adjudication a final decision on a legal matter or a court case

probation a system that allows a criminal to leave prison early or not to go to prison at all, if the person promises to behave well and keeps in contact with a probation officer

parole a system that allows a criminal to leave prison if the person agrees to behave well outside of prison

drunkard someone who drinks too much alcohol and cannot think or act normally

prostitute someone who has sex with people to earn money

smuggle take someone or something illegally from one place to another

narcotics any illegal or unlawfully possessed drug, including marijuana and heroin

gamble to try to win money by playing cards, guessing the result of a race or game, etc.

alimony money that you have to pay regularly to your former wife or husband after a divorce

Part 10. Additional Questions *(Continued)*	Write your USCIS A-Number here: A

E. Removal, Exclusion, and Deportation Proceedings.

25. Are removal, exclusion, rescission, or deportation proceedings pending against you? ☐ Yes ☐ No

26. Have you **ever** been removed, excluded, or deported from the United States? ☐ Yes ☐ No

27. Have you **ever** been ordered to be removed, excluded, or deported from the United States? ☐ Yes ☐ No

28. Have you **ever** applied for any kind of relief from removal, exclusion, or deportation? ☐ Yes ☐ No

F. Military Service.

29. Have you **ever** served in the U.S. Armed Forces? ☐ Yes ☐ No

30. Have you **ever** left the United States to avoid being drafted into the U.S. Armed Forces? ☐ Yes ☐ No

31. Have you **ever** applied for any kind of exemption from military service in the U.S. Armed Forces? ☐ Yes ☐ No

32. Have you **ever** deserted from the U.S. Armed Forces? ☐ Yes ☐ No

G. Selective Service Registration.

33. Are you a male who lived in the United States at any time between your 18th and 26th birthdays in any status except as a lawful nonimmigrant? ☐ Yes ☐ No

If you answered "NO," go on to question 34.

If you answered "YES," provide the information below.

If you answered "YES," but you did not register with the Selective Service System and are still under 26 years of age, you must register before you apply for naturalization, so that you can complete the information below:

Date Registered (mm/dd/yyyy) [   ]   Selective Service Number [   ]

If you answered "YES," but you did not register with the Selective Service and you are now 26 years old or older, attach a statement explaining why you did not register.

H. Oath Requirements. *(See Part 14 for the text of the oath)*

Answer Questions 34 through 39. If you answer "No" to any of these questions, attach (1) your written explanation why the answer was "No" and (2) any additional information or documentation that helps to explain your answer.

34. Do you support the Constitution and form of government of the United States? ☐ Yes ☐ No

35. Do you understand the full Oath of Allegiance to the United States? ☐ Yes ☐ No

36. Are you willing to take the full Oath of Allegiance to the United States? ☐ Yes ☐ No

37. If the law requires it, are you willing to bear arms on behalf of the United States? ☐ Yes ☐ No

38. If the law requires it, are you willing to perform noncombatant services in the U.S. Armed Forces? ☐ Yes ☐ No

39. If the law requires it, are you willing to perform work of national importance under civilian direction? ☐ Yes ☐ No

Form N-400 (Rev. 04/05/10) Y Page 9

---

removal, exclusion, and deportation proceedings the formal process that happens when a non-citizen must leave the United States because the government believes the person is not entitled to be in the country, is illegally in the country, or has violated immigration laws

draft when the government informs you that you must join the military for a period of time

exemption special permission not to do something

desert leave the army without permission

Selective Service an agency of the U.S. government that requires that all male U.S. citizens register with the government within 30 days of their 18th birthday in the event of a national emergency; foreign males between the ages of 18 and 25 living in the United States must also register.

documentation records or papers that show something is true

Oath of Allegiance a formal and serious promise to be loyal to the country

bear arms carry a gun or other military weapons

perform noncombatant services do work with the Armed Forces that does not involve fighting

perform work of national importance do work that is important to the country

Part 11. Your Signature

Write your USCIS A-Number here:
A

I certify, under ==penalty== of ==perjury== under the laws of the United States of America, that this application, and the evidence submitted with it, are all true and correct. I ==authorize the release of any information== that the USCIS needs to determine my eligibility for naturalization.

Your Signature

Date *(mm/dd/yyyy)*

Part 12. Signature of Person Who Prepared This Application for You *(If applicable)*

I declare under penalty of perjury that I prepared this application at the request of the above person. The answers provided are based on information of which I have personal knowledge and/or were provided to me by the above named person in response to the *exact questions* contained on this form.

Preparer's Printed Name

Preparer's Signature

Date *(mm/dd/yyyy)*

Preparer's Firm or Organization Name *(If applicable)*

Preparer's Daytime Phone Number

Preparer's Address - Street Number and Name

City

State

Zip Code

NOTE: Do not complete Parts 13 and 14 until a USCIS Officer instructs you to do so.

Part 13. Signature at Interview

I swear (affirm) and certify under penalty of perjury under the laws of the United States of America that I know that the contents of this application for naturalization subscribed by me, including corrections numbered 1 through _____ and the evidence submitted by me numbered pages 1 through _____, are true and correct to the best of my knowledge and belief.

==Subscribed== to and sworn to (affirmed) before me

Officer's Printed Name or Stamp

Date *(mm/dd/yyyy)*

Complete Signature of Applicant

Officer's Signature

Part 14. Oath of Allegiance

If your application is approved, you will be scheduled for a public oath ceremony at which time you will be required to take the following Oath of Allegiance immediately prior to becoming a naturalized citizen. By signing, you acknowledge your willingness and ability to take this oath:

I hereby declare, on oath, that I absolutely and entirely ==renounce== and abjure all ==allegiance== and ==fidelity== to any foreign prince, ==potentate==, state, or ==sovereignty==, of whom or which I have heretofore been a subject or citizen;

that I will support and defend the Constitution and laws of the United States of America against all enemies, foreign and ==domestic==;

that I will ==bear true faith== and allegiance to the same;

that I will bear arms on behalf of the United States when required by the law;

that I will perform noncombatant service in the Armed Forces of the United States when required by the law;

that I will perform work of national importance under civilian direction when required by the law; and

that I take this obligation freely, without any mental reservation or purpose of ==evasion==, so help me God.

Printed Name of Applicant

Complete Signature of Applicant

Form N-400 (Rev. 04/05/10) Y Page 10

---

penalty punishment

perjury the crime of telling a lie under oath

authorize the release of information give permission to an individual, a group, or an organization to provide facts

subscribe sign your name

renounce say publicly that you no longer believe in or support something

allegiance loyalty to a person, country, or belief

fidelity being faithful and loyal

potentate a ruler with direct power over his or her people

sovereignty an independent country or government

domestic relating to things that happen inside a country

bear true faith to believe in and to follow

evasion the act of deliberately avoiding a duty or question

MAP OF NORTH AMERICA

UNIT 1 LESSON 1

Page 4 Exercise 3

1. a 5. a
2. a 6. a
3. a 7. b
4. b 8. a

Page 4 Exercise 4B

1. T
2. F; Possible answers: Three large tribes were the Cherokee, Seminole, and Sioux.
3. T
4. F; Colonists left Europe to escape persecution.
5. T
6. F; Half of the Pilgrims died during the first winter.
7. T
8. F; The first Thanksgiving was celebrated in America.

Page 6 Exercise 5

People Left Europe to Escape
persecution; political problems
People Came to America to Have
economic opportunity; freedom; land; political liberty; religious freedom

UNIT 1 LESSON 2

Page 7 Exercise 2

Possible answers: The thirteen colonies were all on the East coast / near the ocean. Maine was part of the colony of Massachusetts.

Page 8 Exercise 3A

1. c 2. d 3. a 4. b

Page 8 Exercise 3B

1. self-government
2. taxes
3. original
4. laws

Page 8 Exercise 4B

1. July 4
2. self-government
3. representation
4. army
5. taxes
6. original

Page 10 Exercise 5

a. 6 b. 2 c. 1 d. 3 e. 7 f. 5 g. 4

UNIT 1 LESSON 3

Page 11 Exercise 2

Benjamin Franklin, John Adams, and Thomas Jefferson. Possible answers: They were early leaders of America. They wrote the Declaration of Independence. They helped create a democratic government.

Page 12 Exercise 3

1. b 2. b 3. a 4. a 5. a

Page 12 Exercise 4B

1. independent
2. equal
3. liberty
4. government
5. rights

Page 14 Exercise 5

1. F; Thomas Jefferson wrote the Declaration of Independence.
2. F; The Declaration of Independence was adopted on July 4, 1776.
3. F; July 4 is called "Independence Day."
4. T
5. F; The Declaration of Independence said that all people have the right to life, liberty, and the pursuit of happiness.
6. T
7. F; Jefferson said the job of the government is to protect people's basic rights.

UNIT 1 LESSON 4

Page 15 Exercise 2

Possible answers: A group of men are presenting a paper to the man in the chair. The paper is the Constitution.

Page 16 Exercise 3

1. a 2. a 3. a 4. a 5. b

Page 16 Exercise 4B

1. a 2. b 3. b 4. b 5. a 6. b

Page 18 Exercise 5

a. 2 e. 3
b. 1 f. 7
c. 5 g. 6
d. 4 h. 8

UNIT 1 LESSON 5

Page 19 Exercise 2B

Possible answers: George Washington and Benjamin Franklin are on stamps and bills because they were important leaders in the United States. The U.S. government honors Washington and Franklin for all the work they did to fight for independence and to create a democratic government.

Page 20 Exercise 3B

1. b   2. d   3. a   4. e   5. f   6. c

Page 20 Exercise 4B

1. Constitutional Convention
2. diplomat
3. President
4. Postmaster General
5. Father of Our Country
6. Poor Richard's Almanac

Page 22 Exercise 5

1. GW
2. BF
3. GW
4. GW
5. BF
6. GW
7. BF
8. GW
9. BF
10. BF

UNIT 2 LESSON 1

Page 23 Exercise 2B

A. Great Britain   B. Mexico   C. France
D. Mexico   E. Great Britain   F. Spain

Page 24 Exercise 3B

1. c   2. e   3. a   4. b   5. f   6. d

Page 24 Exercise 4B

Land Through Agreements: Alaska, Louisiana, Florida, Oregon, Washington, Hawaii
Land Through Wars: California, Nevada, Utah, Cuba, Puerto Rico, Guam, the Philippines

Page 26 Exercise 5

Name of War	Involved	Years
War of 1812	United States and Great Britain	1812-1815
Mexican-American War	United States and Mexico	1846-1848
the Civil War	U.S. Northern and Southern states	1861-1865
Spanish-American War	United States and Spain	1898

UNIT 2 LESSON 2

Page 27 Exercise 2

Possible answers: The two pictures show slaves in the United States. Picture on top: Slaves were taken from Africa/their homes; they were forced on a ship to go to the U.S.; they will be sold to slave owners. Picture on bottom: Plantation/slave owners and slaves; they are on a plantation.

Page 28 Exercise 3B

1. b   2. f   3. e   4. a   5. c   6. d

Page 28 Exercise 4B

1. South
2. South
3. North
4. South
5. North
6. South
7. South
8. North
9. North
10. North
11. South

Page 30 Exercise 5

1. F; Abraham Lincoln was President of the United States during the Civil War.
2. T
3. T
4. F; The Southern states depended on slavery for their economy and the Northern states depended on small family farms and factories for their economy.
5. T
6. T
7. F; Most Northern states had laws against slavery.
8. F; The Civil War is also called "the War between the States."
9. F; Large Southern plantations depended on the free work of slaves.

UNIT 2 LESSON 3

Page 31 Exercise 2

Possible answers: He was a President of the United States; he was President during the Civil War; Lincoln ended slavery in the U.S.; he wanted to keep the United States as one country; he was murdered for trying to help slaves and keep the U.S. together.

Page 32 Exercise 3

1. b   2. a   3. b   4. b   5. a   6. b

Page 32 Exercise 4B

1. Confederacy
2. union
3. Emancipation Proclamation
4. President
5. Thirteenth Amendment

Page 34 Exercise 5

a. 6   b. 2   c. 7   d. 3   e. 4   f. 5   g. 1

UNIT 2 LESSON 4

Page 35 Exercise 2

Possible answers: Both pictures: The women want the right to vote; the women are protesting; Picture on bottom: the women are marching to Washington, D.C.

Page 36 Exercise 3B

1. d   2. b   3. f   4. e   5. c   6. a

Page 36 Exercise 4B

1. c   2. e   3. f   4. a   5. d   6. b

Page 38 Exercise 5

1. T
2. T
3. F; Women did not always have equal rights in the United States.
4. T
5. T
6. F; Susan B. Anthony fought for civil rights and women's rights.
7. F; In the United States, women got the right to vote in 1920.
8. F; The Nineteenth Amendment gave all women the right to vote.

UNIT 3 LESSON 1

Page 39 Exercise 2

1. Woodrow Wilson
2. Dwight D. Eisenhower
3. Franklin D. Roosevelt

Page 40 Exercise 3B

1. e   2. a   3. f   4. b   5. d   6. c

Page 40 Exercise 4B

1. World War I
2. Roosevelt
3. Germany; the United States
4. World War II
5. Eisenhower

Page 42 Exercise 5

World War I
a. 3   b. 1   c. 2
World War II
a. 2   b. 1   c. 3   d. 4
The Great Depression
a. 1   b. 4   c. 3   d. 2

UNIT 3 LESSON 2

Page 43 Exercise 2

1   the United States   6   Kuwait
2   Cuba   7   China
3   Venezuela   8   Vietnam
4   Russia   9   North Korea
5   Iraq

Page 44 Exercise 3B

1. e   2. b   3. d   4. c   5. f   6. a

Page 44 Exercise 4B

1. United States
2. Cold War
3. Korean War; Vietnam War
4. Gulf War

Page 46 Exercise 5

1914-1918   World War I
1939-1945   World War II
1950-1953   the Korean War
1959-1975   the Vietnam War
1990-1991   the Persian Gulf War

UNIT 3 LESSON 3

Page 47 Exercise 2

Possible answers: Martin Luther King, Jr.; MLK; a civil rights leader in the USA; fought for equality in the 1960s; was a leader of nonviolent protests; he was murdered because he wanted equal rights for all.

Page 48 Exercise 3

1. a   2. a   3. b   4. a   5. b   6. b

Page 48 Exercise 4B

1. discrimination
2. civil rights movement
3. equal rights
4. peaceful
5. Rosa Parks

Page 50 Exercise 5

1. b   2. a   3. b   4. b   5. a   6. b

UNIT 3 LESSON 4

Page 51 Exercise 2

Possible answers: Terrorists attacked the United States; planes crashed on 9/11; in NYC two planes hit the World Trade Center; the buildings fell down; thousands of people died in the buildings; the passengers crashed the plane on purpose in Pennsylvania; a plane crashed into the Pentagon building

Page 52 Exercise 3

1. terrorist	3. crash	5. security
2. hijack	4. event	6. military

Page 52 Exercise 4B

1. T
2. F; Terrorists attacked New York, Virginia, and Pennsylvania.
3. F; Four airplanes were involved in the attack.
4. T
5. F; One airplane crashed into the Pentagon in Virginia. OR Two airplanes crashed into the World Trade Center in New York City.
6. T
7. T
8. F; New York City created the expression "If you see something, say something."

Page 54 Exercise 5A

Possible sentences: On September 11, terrorists attacked the United States.; Planes crashed into the Twin Towers in New York City, into the Pentagon, and into a field in Pennsylvania.; The passengers on the plane that crashed in Pennsylvania stopped one of the attacks.; The Department of Homeland Security was created after 9/11.

UNIT 4 LESSON 1

Page 55 Exercise 2

We the People; Possible answers: the words mean that people run the government; that everyone is part of the government

Page 56 Exercise 3

1. a   2. a   3. a   4. b   5. b

Page 56 Exercise 4B

1. a   2. b   3. a   4. b   5. a   6. b   7. b

Page 58 Exercise 5

1. Constitution	5. The rule of law
2. Bill of Rights	6. amendment
3. We the people	7. self-government
4. the Founding Fathers	

UNIT 4 LESSON 2

Page 59 Exercise 2

Possible answers: The people in the pictures are exercising their freedoms/rights. Top left: demonstrators, protestors, workers; they are protesting/demonstrating, they are asking for something/change; Bottom left: news reporters, a politician; asking and answering questions in an interview, giving their opinions; Picture on right: a religious/spiritual woman; she is praying

Page 60 Exercise 3

1. The press	5. Trial
2. Crime	6. Assembly
3. Jury	7. Petition
4. Lawyer	

Page 60 Exercise 4B

Situation 1: freedom of press
Situation 2: freedom of speech
Situation 3: freedom of assembly
Situation 4: freedom of religion

Page 62 Exercise 5

1. F; The first ten amendments of the Constitution are the Bill of Rights.
2. T
3. T
4. F; Freedom of speech means a person can say and write what he or she believes.
5. F; Freedom of assembly means people can have meetings in public.
6. T
7. F; Freedom of the press means newspapers and magazines can print what they want as long as it is true.
8. F; There are several amendments that protect the rights of a person who is arrested.

UNIT 5 LESSON 1

Page 63 Exercise 2A

1. the White House
2. the Capitol
3. the Supreme Court

Page 63 Exercise 2B

The President works in the White House. Congress works in the Capitol. The Justices of the Supreme Court work in the Supreme Court.

Page 64 Exercise 3B
1. c   2. a   3. b   4. f   5. e   6. d   7. g

Page 64 Exercise 4B

	Legislative Branch	Executive Branch	Judicial Branch
Place	Congress, the Capitol	The White House	The Supreme Court
People	representatives, senators	the President, the Vice President	judges

Page 66 Exercise 5
1. three
2. President
3. legislative
4. executive
5. judicial
6. Senate
7. courts
8. Congress

UNIT 5 LESSON 2

Page 67 Exercise 2
Top left: President Barack Obama; he leads the government; Top right: Congress, senators, representatives, the Vice President, the Speaker of the House; they make laws; Bottom: Supreme Court justices, they decide on court cases, legal situations

Page 68 Exercise 3
1. a   2. b   3. b   4. b   5. a   6. b

Page 68 Exercise 4B
1. separation of powers
2. veto
3. legislative branch
4. courts
5. President
6. Supreme Court
7. checks and balances

Page 70 Exercise 5

	Executive Branch	Legislative Branch	Judicial Branch
Appointing a judge to the Supreme Court	✓		
Making laws		✓	
Sending a person to prison			✓

UNIT 6 LESSON 1

Page 71 Exercise 2
Possible answers: to sign bills; to lead the military; to meet with foreign leaders/leaders of other countries

Page 72 Exercise 3B
1. c   2. a   3. e   4. b   5. d

Page 72 Exercise 4B
1. November
2. four
3. eight
4. Commander in Chief
5. executive
6. signs
7. vetoes

Page 74 Exercise 5
a. 8   b. 3   c. 4   d. 1   e. 6   f. 2   g. 7   h. 5

UNIT 6 LESSON 2

Page 75 Exercise 2
Possible answers: Barack Obama/President of the United States; Joe Biden/Vice President of the United States; Nancy Pelosi/Speaker of the House. The President is in charge of the executive branch. The President enforces the laws and is the commander in chief of the military. The Vice President is second-in-command to the President. If the President could not do his or her job the Vice President would take over. The Vice President is also the leader of the Senate. The Speaker of the House leads the House of Representatives and is third-in-command to the President.

Page 76 Exercise 3B
1. b   2. e   3. d   4. c   5. a

Page 76 Exercise 4B
1. executive
2. second
3. legislative
4. third
5. Vice President

Page 78 Exercise 5
1. Vice President
2. Speaker of the House
3. Vice President
4. Speaker of the House
5. Speaker of the House
6. Vice President
7. Vice President
8. Vice President

UNIT 6 LESSON 3

Page 79 Exercise 2

Possible answers: Each person in the Cabinet has a different responsibility and a different area of expertise; The President needs so many people in the Cabinet to properly fulfill all the responsibilities and help run the nation.

Page 80 Exercise 3

1. a   2. b   3. a   4. a   5. a   6. b

Page 80 Exercise 4B

1. Cabinet
2. Treasury
3. Defense
4. Attorney General
5. State
6. Agriculture
7. Labor
8. Education
9. Homeland Security

Page 82 Exercise 5

1. T
2. T
3. F; The President chooses the people for the Cabinet.
4. T
5. T
6. F; Cabinet members are part of the executive branch of the government.
7. F; The Secretary of State advises the President on international issues and represents the United States to the world. OR The Secretary of the Treasury advises the President on the economy.
8. T

UNIT 7 LESSON 1

Page 83 Exercise 2

The Capitol building; Washington, D.C.

Page 84 Exercise 3B

1. b   2. c   3. d   4. a   5. e

Page 84 Exercise 4B

1. Congress
2. Senate
3. senators
4. territories
5. bill
6. pass

Page 86 Exercise 5A

1. two
2. 100
3. six years
4. there are no term limits; if a senator continues to be elected to the Senate he or she can continue to serve
5. citizens of the senator's state

Page 86 Exercise 5B

a. 6   b. 1   c. 2   d. 5   e. 3   f. 4

UNIT 7 LESSON 2

Page 87 Exercise 2

The House of Representatives in Congress

Page 88 Exercise 3

1. b   2. a   3. a   4. b   5. b

Page 88 Exercise 4B

1. legislative branch
2. House of Representatives
3. representatives
4. district
5. census
6. population
7. Delegates

Page 90 Exercise 5

1. c   2. a   3. b   4. b   5. c   6. a

UNIT 7 LESSON 3

Page 91 Exercise 2

the Supreme Court; Washington, D.C.

Page 92 Exercise 3B

1. c   2. g   3. b   4. e   5. d   6. f   7. a

Page 92 Exercise 4B

1. judicial branch
2. review
3. Supreme Court
4. justices
5. Constitution
6. President

Page 94 Exercise 5

1. T
2. F; The decision of the Supreme Court is final.
3. F; The President appoints justices to the Supreme Court and the Senate approves them.
4. T
5. F; Once appointed, a justice serves for life or until his or her retirement.
6. T
7. T
8. F; Each justice can vote his or her own way on a case and the justices do not always all agree.

UNIT 8 LESSON 1

Page 95 Exercise 2

Possible answers: Federal government: print money, create an army; State government: education, police protection

Page 96 Exercise 3

1. a   2. b   3. b   4. a   5. b   6. a

Page 96 Exercise 4B

1. Federal
2. State
3. State
4. Federal
5. State
6. State
7. Federal
8. State

Page 98 Exercise 5

1. b   2. b   3. a   4. b   5. a   6. a

UNIT 8 LESSON 2

Page 100 Exercise 3B

1. c   2. d   3. b   4. e   5. a

Page 100 Exercise 4B

1. governor   4. capital
2. legislative   5. taxes
3. federal   6. elect

Page 102 Exercise 5

1. F; Each state has its own laws.
2. T
3. T
4. F; The governor is the head of the executive branch of a state.
5. F; State senators work in the state capital.
6. T
7. T
8. F; States can have different types of taxes.
9. F; The state capital is home to the state government.

UNIT 8 LESSON 3

Page 103 Exercise 2

The voter chose (voted for) the Republican candidates John McCain and Sarah Palin.

Page 104 Exercise 3B

1. e   2. c   3. a   4. b   5. d

Page 104 Exercise 4B

1. Democratic   4. Election Day
2. Republican   5. party members
3. Primary Election   6. citizens

Page 106 Exercise 5

1. c   2. a   3. a   4. a   5. b   6. c

UNIT 9 LESSON 1

Page 107 Exercise 2

Picture on left: A woman is signing a petition. Picture on top right: People are voting in an election. Picture on bottom right: The people are praying/practicing their religion.

Page 108 Exercise 3B

1. run for office   4. worship
2. amendments   5. apply
3. supreme   6. federal

Page 108 Exercise 4B

1. d   2. a   3. e   4. c   5. b

Page 110 Exercise 5

1. Everyone   6. Everyone
2. Citizens   7. Everyone
3. Everyone   8. Citizens
4. Citizens   9. Citizens
5. Everyone   10. Everyone

UNIT 9 LESSON 2

Page 111 Exercise 2

Possible answers: Picture on left: People/volunteers are painting a mural (a wall). They are helping their community. Picture on top right: A politician (Bill Clinton) is talking/listening to people. Picture on bottom right: People/volunteers are working on a political campaign to help elect John McCain and Sarah Palin for President and Vice President (2008).

Page 112 Exercise 3B

1. c   2. a   3. d   4. f   5. e   6. b

Page 112 Exercise 4B

1. jury
2. civic groups
3. federal
4. elected officials
5. Selective Service
6. defend

Page 114 Exercise 5

1. T
2. T
3. F; Only U.S. citizens serve on a jury.
4. F; All men who are at least eighteen years old must register for Selective Service.
5. F; Taxes pay for schools, roads, police, and firefighters.
6. F; The last day you can send in a federal income tax form is April 15.
7. T
8. T

UNIT 10 LESSON 1

Page 116 Exercise 3B

1. b   2. c   3. d   4. e   5. a

Page 116 Exercise 4B

U.S. territories: American Samoa; Guam; Northern Mariana Islands; Puerto Rico; U.S. Virgin Islands
Oceans: Atlantic; Pacific
Rivers: Mississippi; Missouri

Page 118 Exercise 5

1. Possible answers: Maine, New Hampshire, Vermont, New York, Pennsylvania, Ohio, Michigan, Minnesota, North Dakota, Montana, Idaho, Washington, and Alaska
2. Possible answers: California, Arizona, New Mexico, Texas
3. The Mississippi River and the Missouri River
4. Atlantic Ocean
5. Pacific Ocean

UNIT 11 LESSON 1

Page 119 Exercise 2

Possible answers: Many people come to see the Statue of Liberty because it is a symbol of freedom; it is a historical site; they want to see what their relatives saw when they first arrived in the United States

Page 120 Exercise 3

1. a   2. a   3. a   4. b   5. a

Page 120 Exercise 4B

1. Declaration of Independence
2. Statue of Liberty
3. symbol
4. New York harbor

Page 122 Exercise 5

1. France
2. The 100-year anniversary of the Declaration of Independence
3. In New York harbor on Liberty Island
4. over 12 million
5. By boat
6. 354

UNIT 11 LESSON 2

Page 123 Exercise 2

Top left: the flag is in a classroom/in a school; students are saying the Pledge of Allegiance; Bottom left: the flag is on a federal building; all federal buildings fly the American flag. Right: the flag is flying outside/in a park/in a cemetery; the flag is flying at half-staff to remember/to show respect for someone who has died

Page 124 Exercise 3

1. a   2. b   3. b   4. a   5. a

Page 124 Exercise 4B

1. red, white, and blue
2. colonies
3. star
4. "The Star-Spangled Banner"
5. Pledge of Allegiance

Page 126 Exercise 5

1. a   2. a   3. b   4. a   5. b   6. b

UNIT 12 LESSON 1

Page 127 Exercise 2

1. fireworks   2. parade   3. barbecue

Page 128 Exercise 3B

1. e   2. c   3. b   4. a   5. d

Page 128 Exercise 4B

1. January
2. January
3. February
4. May
5. June
6. July
7. September
8. October
9. November
10. November
11. December

Page 130 Exercise 5

1. i   2. f   3. c   4. h   5. a
6. b   7. g   8. e   9. d

UNIT 1 LESSON 1

Page 132 Exercise 1A

a

Page 132 Exercise 1B

a

Page 132 Exercise 1C

1. they are
2. he isn't
3. they weren't
4. she wasn't
5. I am

Page 133 Exercise 2A

1. I do
2. I did
3. I do
4. I don't
5. I didn't

Page 133 Exercise 2B

1. B: I am; B: I didn't; B: I do; B: I do
2. B: I am; B: I am; B: she does

UNIT 1 LESSON 2

Page 134 Exercise 1A

b

Page 134 Exercise 1B

1. A: isn't; B: it is
2. A: weren't; B: they were
3. A: doesn't; B: it does
4. A: wasn't; B: it was
5. A: weren't; B: there were

Page 135 Exercise 2

Long answers will vary.
1. A: are you; B: I'm not
2. A: was there; B: there wasn't
3. A: is it; B: it isn't
4. A: did we; B: we didn't
5. A: did you: B: I didn't OR we didn't
6. A: did it; B: it didn't

UNIT 1 LESSON 3

Page 136 Exercise 1A

a

Page 136 Exercise 1B

1. a   2. b   3. b   4. a   5. a

Page 137 Exercise 2A

1. 've taken
2. 's been
3. 've [never] told
4. 've [always] paid
5. have [always] lived

Page 137 Exercise 2B

1. A: brought; B: have
2. A: traveled; B: 've traveled
3. A: served; B: I've [never] served
4. A: come; B: haven't
5. A: visited; B: 've visited
6. A: been married; B: was married

UNIT 1 LESSON 4

Page 138 Exercise 1A

a

Page 138 Exercise 1B

1. How long   3. How long
2. How many   4. How many

Page 138 Exercise 1C

1. b   2. a   3. d   4. c

Page 139 Exercise 2

1. A: How long; B: 've lived
2. A: How many; B: 've moved
3. A: How long; B: 've worked
4. A: How long
5. A: How many
6. A: How many; B: 've taken
7. A: how many
8. A: How long; B: 've been

UNIT 2 LESSON 1

Page 140 Exercise 1A

Answers will vary.

Page 140 Exercise 2A

2 (I am Manuel Vega.)
4 (I am a USCIS Immigration Services officer.)

Page 140 Exercise 2B

1. a   2. b

Page 141 Exercise 3C

1 (She stood up.), 3 (She made eye contact.), 5 (She smiled.)

UNIT 2 LESSON 2

Page 142 Exercise 2A

1 (the weather), 5 (finding the USCIS office), 7 (traffic)

Page 142 Exercise 2B

1. b   2. a   3. b

Page 143 Exercise 3B

2 (She only talks about appropriate topics.)

UNIT 2 LESSON 3

Page 144 Exercise 2A

2 (Please come in.), 3 (Would you like to hang up your coat?), 5 (Can you raise your right hand?)

Page 144 Exercise 2B

a. 6   b. 3   c. 2   d. 1   e. 4   f. 5

Page 145 Exercise 3B

1. b   2. b   3. a   4. a   5. b   6. a

Page 145 Exercise 3C

Possible answers:
1. A: Please come in.   B: Thank you.
2. A: Please hang up your coat.   B: OK. Thank you.

UNIT 2 LESSON 4

Page 146 Exercise 2A

1. F   2. T   3. T   4. F

Page 146 Exercise 2B

Because, love, a lot, freedom

Page 147 Exercise 3B

1 (She sits up straight when listening to questions.), 3 (She seems interested in the questions.), 4 (She looks the officer in the eye.)

UNIT 3 LESSON 1

Page 148 Exercise 2A

a

Page 148 Exercise 2B

1. F   2. F   3. T

Page 149 Exercise 3A

b

UNIT 3 LESSON 2

Page 150 Exercise 2A

Mrs. Rivas did not give her marital status.

Page 150 Exercise 2B

1. b   2. b   3. c   4. b   5. a

Page 151 Exercise 3A

1. b   2. a

UNIT 3 LESSON 3

Page 152 Exercise 2A

Yes. She is a receptionist in a doctor's office.

Page 152 Exercise 2B

1. b   2. a   3. b   4. b   5. a

Page 153 Exercise 3A

a

UNIT 3 LESSON 4

Page 154 Exercise 2A

No

Page 154 Exercise 2B

1. b   2. b   3. a   4. c

Page 155 Exercise 3A

1. Let me think.   2. One minute please.

UNIT 3 LESSON 5

Page 156 Exercise 2A

Mrs. Rivas has been married one time.

Page 156 Exercise 2B

1. F   2. T   3. F   4. F   5. T

Page 157 Exercise 3A

citizenship

UNIT 3 LESSON 6

Page 158 Exercise 2A

No. She did not list her oldest son, Arturo Junior.

Page 158 Exercise 2B

1. a   2. b   3. a   4. b

Page 159 Exercise 3A

a

UNIT 4 LESSON 1

Page 160 Exercise 2A

Yes, Mr. Gao pays his taxes.

Page 160 Exercise 2B

1. b   2. a   3. b   4. a

Page 161 Exercise 3A

Excuse me.

UNIT 4 LESSON 2

Page 162 Exercise 2A

Yes, a restaurant association.

Page 162 Exercise 2B

1. b   2. b   3. a

Page 163 Exercise 3A

b

UNIT 4 LESSON 3

Page 164 Exercise 2A

No

Page 164 Exercise 2B

1 (committed a crime or offence for which you were not arrested), 3 (been arrested), 4 (been cited), 5 (been detained)

Page 165 Exercise 3A

I have never been detained.

UNIT 4 LESSON 4

Page 166 Exercise 2A

Yes

Page 166 Exercise 2B

1. F   2. T   3. F   4. T

Page 167 Exercise 3A

Mr. Gao answers with *yes*, *no*, or very short answers.

UNIT 4 LESSON 5

Page 168 Exercise 2A

Mr. Gao has been practicing the oath at home.

Page 168 Exercise 2B

1. T   2. T   3. F   4. T   5. F

Page 169 Exercise 3A

b

UNIT 4 LESSON 6

Page 170 Exercise 3

1. a   2. a   3. a   4. b   5. b   6. b

Page 171 Exercise 4A

The Oath of Allegiance

I hereby declare, / on oath, / that I absolutely and entirely renounce and abjure / all allegiance and fidelity / to any foreign prince, potentate, state, or sovereignty, / of whom or which I have heretofore been a subject or citizen; / that I will support and defend the Constitution and laws of the United States of America / against all enemies, / foreign and domestic; / that I will bear true faith and allegiance to the same; / that I will bear arms on behalf of the United States / when required by the law; / that I will perform noncombatant service in the armed forces of the United States / when required by the law; / and that I take this obligation freely, / without any mental reservation / or purpose of evasion, / so help me God.

1. What is the supreme law of the land?
   - *the Constitution*

2. What does the Constitution do?
   - *sets up the government*
   - *defines the government*
   - *protects basic rights of Americans*

3. The idea of self-government is in the first three words of the Constitution. What are these words?
   - *We the People*

4. What is an amendment?
   - *a change to the Constitution*
   - *an addition to the Constitution*

5. What do we call the first ten amendments to the Constitution?
   - *the Bill of Rights*

6. What is <u>one</u> right or freedom from the First Amendment?
   - *speech*
   - *religion*
   - *assembly*
   - *press*
   - *petition the government*

7. How many amendments does the Constitution have?
   - *twenty-seven (27)*

8. What did the Declaration of Independence do?
   - *announced our independence from Great Britain*
   - *declared our independence from Great Britain*
   - *said that the United States is free from Great Britain*

9. What are <u>two</u> rights in the Declaration of Independence?
   - *life*
   - *liberty*
   - *pursuit of happiness*

10. What is freedom of religion?
    - *You can practice any religion, or not practice a religion.*

11. What is the economic system in the United States?
    - *capitalist economy*
    - *market economy*

12. What is the "rule of law"?
    - *Everyone must follow the law.*
    - *Leaders must obey the law.*
    - *Government must obey the law.*
    - *No one is above the law.*

13. Name <u>one</u> branch, or part, of the government.
    - *Congress*
    - *legislative*
    - *President*
    - *executive*
    - *the courts*
    - *judicial*

14. What stops <u>one</u> branch of government from becoming too powerful?
    - *checks and balances*
    - *separation of powers*

15. Who is in charge of the executive branch?
    - *the President*

16. Who makes federal laws?
    - *Congress*
    - *Senate and House of Representatives*
    - *U.S. or national legislature*

17. What are the <u>two</u> parts of the U.S. Congress?
    - *the Senate and House of Representatives*

18. How many U.S. Senators are there?
    - *one hundred (100)*

19. We elect a U.S. Senator for how many years?
    - *six (6)*

20. Who is <u>one</u> of your state's U.S. Senators now?
    - *Check the government website for your state.*

21. The House of Representatives has how many voting members?
    - *four hundred thirty-five (435)*

22. We elect a U.S. Representative for how many years?
    - *two (2)*

23. Name your U.S. Representative.
    - *Check the government website for your state.*

24. Who does a U.S. Senator represent?
    - *all people of the state*

25. Why do some states have more Representatives than other states?
    - *because of the state's population*
    - *because they have more people*
    - *because some states have more people*

26. We elect a President for how many years?
    - *four (4)*

27. In what month do we vote for President?
    - *November*

28. What is the name of the President of the United States now?
    - *Barack H. Obama*
    - *Barack Obama*
    - *Obama*

29. What is the name of the Vice President of the United States now?
    - *Joseph Biden*
    - *Joe Biden*
    - *Biden*

30. If the President can no longer serve, who becomes President?
    - *the Vice President*

31. If both the President and the Vice President can no longer serve, who becomes President?
    - *the Speaker of the House*

32. Who is the Commander in Chief of the military?
    - *the President*

33. Who signs bills to become laws?
    - *the President*

34. Who vetoes bills?
    - *the President*

35. What does the President's Cabinet do?
    - *advises the President*

36. What are two Cabinet-level positions?
    - *Secretary of Agriculture*
    - *Secretary of Commerce*
    - *Secretary of Defense*
    - *Secretary of Education*
    - *Secretary of Energy*
    - *Secretary of Health and Human Services*
    - *Secretary of Homeland Security*
    - *Secretary of Housing and Urban Development*
    - *Secretary of the Interior*
    - *Secretary of Labor*
    - *Secretary of State*
    - *Secretary of Transportation*
    - *Secretary of the Treasury*
    - *Secretary of Veterans Affairs*
    - *Attorney General*
    - *Vice President*

37. What does the judicial branch do?
    - *reviews law*
    - *explains law*
    - *resolves disputes or disagreements*
    - *decides if a law goes against the Constitution*

38. What is the highest court in the United States?
    - *the Supreme Court*

39. How many justices are on the Supreme Court?
    - *nine (9)*

40. Who is the Chief Justice of the United States now?
    - *John Roberts*
    - *John G. Roberts, Jr.*

41. Under our Constitution, some powers belong to the federal government. What is <u>one</u> power of the federal government?
    - *to print money*
    - *to declare war*
    - *to create an army*
    - *to make treaties*

42. Under our Constitution, some powers belong to the states. What is <u>one</u> power of the states?
    - *provide schooling and education*
    - *provide protection (police)*
    - *provide safety (fire departments)*
    - *give a driver's license*
    - *approve zoning and land use*

43. Who is the Governor of your state now?
    - *Check the government website for your state.*

44. What is the capital of your state?
    - *Check the government website for your state.*

45. What are the <u>two</u> major political parties in the United States?
    - *Democratic and Republican*

46. What is the political party of the President now?
    - *Democratic Party*

47. What is the name of the Speaker of the House of Representatives now?
    - *John Boehner*

48. There are four amendments to the Constitution about who can vote. Describe <u>one</u> of them.
    - *Citizens eighteen (18) and older can vote.*
    - *You don't have to pay a poll tax to vote.*
    - *Any citizen can vote. (Women and men can vote.)*
    - *A male citizen of any race can vote.*

49. What is <u>one</u> responsibility that is only for United States citizens?
    - *serve on a jury*
    - *vote in a federal election*

50. Name <u>one</u> right only for United States citizens.
    - *vote in a federal election*
    - *run for federal office*

51. What are <u>two</u> rights of everyone living in the United States?
    - *freedom of expression*
    - *freedom of speech*
    - *freedom of assembly*
    - *freedom to petition the government*
    - *freedom of worship*
    - *the right to bear arms*

52. What do we show loyalty to when we say the Pledge of Allegiance?
    - *the United States*
    - *the flag*

53. What is <u>one</u> promise you make when you become a United States citizen?
    - *give up loyalty to other countries*
    - *defend the Constitution and laws of the United States*
    - *obey the laws of the United States*
    - *serve in the U.S. military if needed*
    - *serve (do important work for) the nation if needed*
    - *be loyal to the United States*

54. How old do citizens have to be to vote for President?
    - *eighteen (18) and older*

55. What are <u>two</u> ways that Americans can participate in their democracy?
    - *vote*
    - *join a political party*
    - *help with a campaign*
    - *join a civic group*
    - *join a community group*
    - *give an elected official your opinion on an issue*
    - *call Senators and Representatives*
    - *publicly support or oppose an issue or policy*
    - *run for office*
    - *write to a newspaper*

56. When is the last day you can send in federal income tax forms?
    - *April 15*

57. When must all men register for the Selective Service?
    - *at age eighteen (18)*
    - *between eighteen (18) and twenty-six (26)*

58. What is <u>one</u> reason colonists came to America?
    - *freedom*
    - *political liberty*
    - *religious freedom*
    - *economic opportunity*
    - *practice their religion*
    - *escape persecution*

59. Who lived in America before the Europeans arrived?
    - *American Indians*
    - *Native Americans*

60. What group of people was taken to America and sold as slaves?
    - *Africans*
    - *people from Africa*

61. Why did the colonists fight the British?
    - *because of high taxes (taxation without representation)*
    - *because the British army stayed in their houses (boarding, quartering)*
    - *because they didn't have self-government*

62. Who wrote the Declaration of Independence?
    - *(Thomas) Jefferson*

63. When was the Declaration of Independence adopted?
    - *July 4, 1776*

64. There were 13 original states. Name <u>three</u>.
    - *New Hampshire*
    - *Massachusetts*
    - *Rhode Island*
    - *Connecticut*
    - *New York*
    - *New Jersey*
    - *Pennsylvania*
    - *Delaware*
    - *Maryland*
    - *Virginia*
    - *North Carolina*
    - *South Carolina*
    - *Georgia*

65. What happened at the Constitutional Convention?
    - *The Constitution was written.*
    - *The Founding Fathers wrote the Constitution.*

66. When was the Constitution written?
    - *1787*

67. The Federalist Papers supported the passage of the U.S. Constitution. Name <u>one</u> of the writers.
    - *(James) Madison*
    - *(Alexander) Hamilton*
    - *(John) Jay*
    - *Publius*

68. What is <u>one</u> thing Benjamin Franklin is famous for?
    - *U.S. diplomat*
    - *oldest member of the Constitutional Convention*
    - *first Postmaster General of the United States*
    - *writer of "Poor Richard's Almanac"*
    - *started the first free libraries*

69. Who is the "Father of Our Country"?
    - *(George) Washington*

70. Who was the first President?
    - *(George) Washington*

71. What territory did the United States buy from France in 1803?
    - *the Louisiana Territory*
    - *Louisiana*

72. Name <u>one</u> war fought by the United States in the 1800s.
    - *War of 1812*
    - *Mexican-American War*
    - *Civil War*
    - *Spanish-American War*

73. Name the U.S. war between the North and the South.
    - *the Civil War*
    - *the War between the States*

74. Name <u>one</u> problem that led to the Civil War.
    - *slavery*
    - *economic reasons*
    - *states' rights*

75. What was <u>one</u> important thing that Abraham Lincoln did?
    - *freed the slaves (Emancipation Proclamation)*
    - *saved (or preserved) the Union*
    - *led the United States during the Civil War*

76. What did the Emancipation Proclamation do?
    - *freed the slaves*
    - *freed slaves in the Confederacy*
    - *freed slaves in the Confederate states*
    - *freed slaves in most Southern states*

77. What did Susan B. Anthony do?
    - *fought for women's rights*
    - *fought for civil rights*

78. Name <u>one</u> war fought by the United States in the 1900s.
    - *World War I*
    - *World War II*
    - *Korean War*
    - *Vietnam War*
    - *Persian Gulf War*

79. Who was President during World War I?
    - *(Woodrow) Wilson*

80. Who was President during the Great Depression and World War II?
    - *(Franklin) Roosevelt*

81. Who did the United States fight in World War II?
    - *Japan, Germany, and Italy*

82. Before he was President, Eisenhower was a general. What war was he in?
    - *World War II*

83. During the Cold War, what was the main concern of the United States?
    - *Communism*

84. What movement tried to end racial discrimination?
    - *civil rights movement*

85. What did Martin Luther King, Jr. do?
    - *fought for civil rights*
    - *worked for equality for all Americans*

86. What major event happened on September 11, 2001, in the United States?
    - *Terrorists attacked the United States.*

87. Name <u>one</u> American Indian tribe in the United States.
    - *Cherokee*
    - *Navajo*
    - *Sioux*
    - *Chippewa*
    - *Choctaw*
    - *Pueblo*
    - *Apache*
    - *Iroquois*
    - *Creek*
    - *Blackfeet*
    - *Seminole*
    - *Cheyenne*
    - *Arawak*
    - *Shawnee*
    - *Mohegan*
    - *Huron*
    - *Oneida*
    - *Lakota*
    - *Crow*
    - *Teton*
    - *Hopi*
    - *Inuit*

88. Name <u>one</u> of the two longest rivers in the United States.
    - *Missouri River*
    - *Mississippi River*

89. What ocean is on the West Coast of the United States?
    - *Pacific Ocean*

90. What ocean is on the East Coast of the United States?
- *Atlantic Ocean*

91. Name <u>one</u> U.S. territory.
- *Puerto Rico*
- *U.S. Virgin Islands*
- *American Samoa*
- *Northern Mariana Islands*
- *Guam*

92. Name <u>one</u> state that borders Canada.
- *Maine*
- *New Hampshire*
- *Vermont*
- *New York*
- *Pennsylvania*
- *Ohio*
- *Michigan*
- *Minnesota*
- *North Dakota*
- *Montana*
- *Idaho*
- *Washington*
- *Alaska*

93. Name <u>one</u> state that borders Mexico.
- *California*
- *Arizona*
- *New Mexico*
- *Texas*

94. What is the capital of the United States?
- *Washington, D.C.*

95. Where is the Statue of Liberty?
- *New York Harbor*
- *Liberty Island*
- *New Jersey*
- *near New York City*
- *on the Hudson River*

96. Why does the flag have 13 stripes?
- *because there were 13 original colonies*
- *because the stripes represent the original colonies*

97. Why does the flag have 50 stars?
- *because there is one star for each state*
- *because each star represents a state*
- *because there are 50 states*

98. What is the name of the national anthem?
- *The Star-Spangled Banner*

99. When do we celebrate Independence Day?
- *July 4*

100. Name <u>two</u> national U.S. holidays.
- *New Year's Day*
- *Martin Luther King, Jr. Day*
- *Presidents' Day*
- *Memorial Day*
- *Independence Day*
- *Labor Day*
- *Columbus Day*
- *Veterans Day*
- *Thanksgiving*
- *Christmas*